Getting the job you want

Howard Dowding
and
Sheila Boyce

Ward Lock Limited · London

First published in Great Britain in 1979
by Ward Lock Limited, 8 Clifford Street,
London W1X 1RB, an Egmont Company.

Revised edition 1982
Reprinted 1983, 1986

Text IBM set in Press Roman medium
by Type Practitioners Ltd, Sevenoaks, Kent.

Printed and bound in Great Britain by
Hollen Street Press Limited

British Library Cataloguing in Publication Data

Dowding, Howard
Getting the job you want.
1. Applications for positions.
I. Title II. Boyce, Sheila
331.1'28 HF5383

ISBN 0-7063-6492-9

Contents

Preface

Every year a large proportion of the working population change their jobs. For the majority of us, changing jobs is a worrying and taxing time. This is not just because of the importance of our jobs but also because we are ill equipped for the job-changing process itself and often leave the result to chance or good luck.

This book is dedicated to the person who wants to better equip himself so as to make success more certain. It is written so that it can be used as a working guide and the points in it reviewed quickly. It is based on the experience of helping many people with their job applications and on lectures given to audiences of job hunters.

Howard L Dowding MSc., ACIS
Sheila M Boyce

1 Introduction

Finding another job is a procedure most people do not undertake often. Most job hunters have little idea of how to go about presenting themselves to prospective employers in the best possible light. This is just as true for senior people as for the average job hunter. Each step in the process must be well thought out, planned and checked. Those people who prepare themselves thoroughly will succeed quickly, those who do not, will have to be content with a long struggle and good luck. The secrets of success are:

- an insight into the job-hunting process
- a careful evaluation of the job you are going after
- selective presentation of your experience and abilities
- careful planning of letters and interviews
- the projection of yourself as a positive personality
- determination to win

Meet as equals Your experience, aptitudes and skills, together with the ability to work are the commodities which you are selling. The employer has facilities to put at your disposal, work to be done and a salary to pay you. He needs you as much as you need him. All negotiations must, therefore, be conducted on the basis that you and the employer meet as equals. Do not feel that you are in an inferior position. If you are the person for the job, it is you who are in the strongest position. Your whole job-hunting campaign must be conducted on the basis that you are selecting one employer from among many possibles – just as the employer is selecting a person from amongst a number of candidates. If you believe this, then your prospective employer will too. Employers like to have people who are in demand, and have confidence in their abilities.

Get organized You are marketing yourself – by yourself. You are your own sales manager, salesman, public relations man, secretary and clerk. You must get organized.

The best jobs are not necessarily obtained by the cleverest or ablest candidates, but by those who plan, get themselves organized and then act. If you are not quite ready to change your job but think that you may do so in say a year's time, why not have a few trial runs by going after 'long shot' jobs, i.e., those which you would be pleased to get but do not think you stand much of a chance of getting. Being successful at job hunting is no different from anything else – it takes time and practice. Do not worry about losing confidence at not getting these jobs – you know they are 'long shots' anyway. You will improve your letter-writing and interview technique. You will also find that your chances of interview steadily increase as your letter-writing ability improves.

You do not have to bare your soul It is customary for you, the job hunter, to feel that you have to disclose everything and answer every question put to you, whereas the employer may exaggerate opportunities and even misrepresent the kind of work which you will be doing. Although you can be quite selective in what you tell your prospective employer, do not be tempted to be dishonest or misrepresent your experience. You must always act honestly and honourably, but make sure that the employer does so as well. Be prepared to cross-check any claims which he may make, but expect that he will do the same for you. Never be tempted to misrepresent your qualifications; there is an increasing tendency for employers to check up on them.

One of the most important criteria by which you will be judged is not what you tell the interviewer, but how you conduct yourself at the interview and approach the job-changing process. Give an impression that you are efficient, business-like and know what you are doing. The interviewer will assume that you approach your job in the same way.

Filling vacancies Filling vacancies is an employer-orientated function; employers place advertisements, retain employment agencies, compile short lists, etc. The employer is in command of the situation. However, you should think of job hunting, not as filling a vacancy for an employer, but as finding an employer for your services. It may be a job as far as the employer is concerned, but for you it is one of the most important aspects of your life.

All too often, job hunters take the attitude that they should be grateful for the job offered and will do anything and suffer any humiliation to get it. The job, in fact, goes to the candidate with the opposite attitude. The employer has a problem because he has a job to be done and needs someone to do it. You will solve his prob-

lem if you convince him that you are the right person for the job.
The employer is not trying to find an outstanding person. But he is worried about hiring someone whom he later finds is incapable of doing the job. All you need do is to convince him that you are capable of doing the job a little better than the other candidates.

It takes time Do not despair if you do not immediately find the job you want. The average times for finding a job are shown below.

Type of job	*Average time to find job*
Non professional, non managerial	1 to 6 months
Professional/junior management	3 to 6 months
Middle management, senior academic	6 to 12 months
Senior management	12 to 24 months

If you follow the advice given in this book you should be successful in much less than the average time.

How to use this book Read this book thoroughly. At each stage of the job hunting process, re-read the relevant chapter, take a copy of the checklist and complete it. Make a point of analysing every section of every chapter to see if the advice contained in it can be applied to you.

If you follow the advice in this book you are bound to be successful, and sooner than you think. The aim of this book is to enable the person, who is qualified, and has the experience to do the job to greatly increase his chances of getting it by outclassing the other candidates both in his letter of application and at interview. It is not written to allow a person not so qualified to charm his way into a job which he does not deserve.

Make a start Get a file to keep your job hunting correspondence in. This will consist of:

- testimonials
- advertisements
- copies of your letters
- correspondence from employers
- checklists
- notes taken after each interview

This file will enable you to make use of previous experience and *Learn from your mistakes.*

2 Finding out about vacancies

There are always thousands of vacancies being created and filled and a few of these are the jobs you want. Just as with a pan of boiling water, new bubbles are continuously being formed, rising to the surface and disappearing – so vacancies are in a constant state of creation and fulfilment. You are, therefore, wasting your time if you wait for your dream job to appear. *The vacancy exists now.* The problem is to track it down. Vacancies occur for the following reasons:

- A general expansion of the organization creating vacancies at all levels.
- Expansion of one particular department, e.g. data processing department creating the need for computer operators, programmers and data control personnel.
- Creation of a new department within the organization, e.g. a market research department within an electronics company.
- Creation of a new specialist job, e.g. leisure officer in a local authority.
- Replacing a person who has been promoted.
- Replacing a person who has left the organization or who has transferred to another department.

Many of these vacancies are not suddenly created; the organizations concerned know that they are going to occur. If you make your approach during this time you may be able to get the job before other people are even considered. This is known as the direct approach and is considered later in this chapter.

The following are the ways through which you can find out about vacancies:

advertisements in newspapers
advertisements in trade and professional journals

government agencies
private agencies and consultancies
executive search consultancies
professional institutions – which may keep registers
Trades Unions – which sometimes keep registers
firms retained by job hunters
the 'old boy' network
approaching employers directly
placing advertisements in professional journals

Use as many of the above ways as possible to give yourself the widest possible coverage.

ADVERTISEMENTS

Only about 40 per cent of vacancies are actually advertised. If, therefore, you rely solely on scanning the daily papers you are severely limiting your horizons. Make sure you read the appropriate trade papers and professional journals to get at all possible advertisements. As well as reading all these advertisements, follow up the other methods of tracking down vacancies as listed above *so as to get at that other 60 per cent.*

AGENCIES

Consultancies and agencies are paid by employers and normally receive a percentage of the first year's salary. Therefore, they are in business to serve employers, not you. They are interested in filling a vacancy for an employer, not finding a job for you – a subtle but important difference. Although they can be very useful, do not place too much faith in them.

Agencies are better for getting you a job similar to your present one rather than one which is different. This is because it is easier to match job descriptions against your existing experience and abilities, rather than your potential wants and ambitions. Agencies like matching job profiles against actual experience profiles, because it is quicker, and requires the least effort on their part. It can also be performed by a relatively junior person.

Do not *rely* on Agencies. Do not expect agencies, etc., to 'keep you in mind' they seldom do. If you do register with an agency, keep pestering them to make sure that they are continuing their efforts to help you. Apart from reviewing your forms once a week or so they only know that you actually exist by you ringing them. Get yourself known to the person who is handling your application. Discuss with him the sort of job which you hope to get. Make yourself stand out from the other people he is handling.

If you are going after a different type of job from your present one, it is even more important to get to know the consultant. You will therefore be able to discuss with him your requirements, and to make sure that he is personally involved with trying to match you with potential jobs.

Never rely solely on an agency. You could find yourself in for a long wait if you do.

FIRMS RETAINED BY JOB HUNTERS

Seek out those firms which work specifically for, and are retained by the job hunter himself. These firms, although few and far between, usually place small advertisements in the classified section of newspapers. They will be able to give you valuable advice and guidance on how you should market yourself. They may also send their own lists of job hunters to employers. These firms are often able to spend a lot of time with you and find out what sort of job would really suit you and give you the relevant advice.

They are more useful than agencies if you are thinking of changing your career. However, you will have to pay for this service, but the time and money spent in counselling sessions will generally be well spent.

THE DIRECT APPROACH

If you approach employers directly – either by writing or telephoning you will have a big advantage over other job hunters. You will probably have no competitors for the job, since with luck, the job will not have been advertised. Any letters sent to a firm must be *individually composed and typed.* Duplicated standard letters will be consigned to the rubbish bin where they belong. However, do not write long detailed letters. Follow the advice on letter writing given in chapter 4. You have only one chance of writing a letter to an employer; if he ignores it, you cannot write another letter or expect a second consideration. Choose your points carefully and make your letter short but give it maximum punch.

WERE YOU SACKED? THEN CLEAR THE AIR

If you were sacked by your previous employer there are three things which you must do:

1) Contact the person who sacked you, and discuss with him what you are now doing. This will reduce any animosity between you and enhance your chances of getting another job, since your previous employer will now be more ready to give you a favourable reference.

2) Check up and find out what your previous employer is saying, or implying about you when acting as a referee. He may well be slandering you even though it is unintentional. For example, you may have been unable to satisfactorily complete a project because training which was promised was never given and funds were withdrawn.

This may have been used as an excuse to sack you and your previous employer could be saying in references that 'you fell down on the job'. In these circumstances you should point out to him that there are laws covering slander and libel, and unless he stops he will be brought to court in an action for damages. This should have the desired effect and any further references he gives will probably be neutral but satisfactory.

3) Always work out your notice. Do not be tempted to take payment in lieu. It is far easier to get another job if you are currently employed. There is a definite prejudice against hiring an unemployed person. You must swallow your pride and continue working as though nothing had happened and still maintain a pleasant working relationship with your manager and colleagues.

REDUNDANT? KEEP YOUR CONFIDENCE

Most redundancies are caused by an underlying contraction of a particular industry or service. If this is so in your case, getting another job in the same field may only be a temporary measure until you are made redundant yet again in a few years time. Consider a complete change of occupation now!

If you are at present employed but redundancy is a possibility, consider a change of career now, and at least start 'unhooking' yourself, both mentally and financially, from your present job. This can be done by finding new interests and earning extra money from a part-time job. Do not make the mistake of becoming more involved with your present job by working even harder and longer hours, since when the end does come and you lose your job, the trauma of it will be much greater.

If you are made redundant, take another job as soon as possible. Consider working freelance, for an agency, or on short term contract. *Never stay at home waiting for something to turn up.* If you continue working even in an entirely different field you will achieve three important objectives:

1) You will raise your morale because you are supporting yourself and have taken a positive step forward.
2) You will be more likely to hear of the kind of job for which you are really looking since you will be in contact with more people.
3) You will enhance your prospect of getting another job since a person in employment is always more desirable than someone who is unemployed.

OUT OF JOB! THEN EMPLOY YOURSELF

As you are definitely more attractive to a future employer if you are employed, consider registering yourself as a business name and using it to employ yourself. Hire yourself out as a consultant to other companies. In your letters of application for jobs you can state that you are working as a consultant and at the interview give your business name as the name of your employer. For instance an unemployed computer programmer called Smith could register a business name called 'Smith Computer Consultants (Programming)' and probably obtain short term work easier than by trying to find it under his own name. Who knows, you may even start your own business this way!

GETTING BACK TO WORK

If you have not been working for some time, e.g. a housewife returning to work, then you must prepare yourself for that first full-time job so as to get the best possible offer. Gaining confidence in yourself is the most difficult task which you face – and one which people who have never given up work do not understand. You need this confidence to convince yourself that you are capable of working for an employer again, both in terms of doing useful work but also in terms of getting back to the discipline of actually going to work. Get involved in working with people, by helping with school fêtes, local charities, etc., and particularly by doing a part-time job. These experiences will start to give you back your confidence and can be drawn upon in your letter of application, and interview.

Consider a few months intensive study on subjects likely to be useful, such as: bookkeeping, languages, taxation, etc. Very often, the person who is successful in their job application is the one who has that little extra knowledge and experience which is useful to the employer.

3 Filling in forms

Many organizations require job applicants to fill in an application form. These forms are often ill-conceived and require a lot of irrelevant information. An application form, for a specific job, should always be returned with a covering letter. Your main effort at securing an interview should be directed to the contents of your letter and not what you state on the form.

Before filling in a form take a copy of it and fill in that as a trial. (Most secretarial agencies have a copying machine which you can use). You can then fill in the actual form without any mistakes or crossings out.

AGENCY FORMS

Employment agencies often ask you to fill in a form which can then be matched against job specifications received from the employers on their books.

When filling in such a form describe the job you want in general terms. The more specific you are, the more you will exclude other jobs which could be suitable. Use space on these forms to cover the type of points you would normally put in a letter. Although a covering letter should also be returned with the form, it may be separated from it when the form is filed at the agency.

After you have sent your forms and letter back to the agency, ring them up and ask to speak to the consultant who is handling your application. In this way you can develop a personal relationship between him and yourself. This will help him to keep you in mind as jobs crop up. This is always very important when you are seeking a job which is of a different type to the one you are now doing.

Job titles You must remember that in many agencies it is a relatively junior person who matches your form against job specifications.

This person, of course, will not be experienced in your field of work. Therefore never use jargon or technical terms. Describe your present job and experience in terms which this person will understand. Do not necessarily put your present job title. Many organizations have their own peculiar job titles which no one else understands. In these circumstances, it is better to invent a job title which will give a better understanding of the job which you do. If the specific job title is required at the interview you can give it then, and explain why you used the one which you actually wrote down on the form. For example the term 'systems engineer' can mean the following:

electronics engineer
project engineer
data processing consultant
systems analyst
technical support person

One of the latter descriptions should be used to give the person reading the form a clearer idea of what you do.

WHAT TO FILL IN AND LEAVE OUT

Do not name your present employer Do not put the name of your present employer since some organizations have a prejudice against employing a person from certain other companies. These could be competitors or similar companies in the same area, etc. In the space provided just mention the type of company it is. For example: 'medium-sized general engineering company' or 'export office'.

Reasons for leaving – must be acceptable Never put your reasons for leaving your present employer. You cannot adequately explain these in a short sentence as required by a form. Acceptable reasons for leaving can be brought up at the interview. These are discussed in chapter 7.

Describe what you hope to be doing in your next job Extract from your present duties those which come closest to the duties you hope to be doing in your next job. You must be quite selective here but do not be dishonest. The golden rule is to at all times write what the prospective employer wants to hear; and obviously he wants to hear your experience in the areas which are appropriate to him.

If you are replying to a specific advertisement, analyse it as shown in chapter 4 and extract from your present duties those which most closely fit the requirements of the job advertisement.

Salary – be careful When filling in agency forms, always quote the largest possible salary range or leave blank. Thus, you will be considered for as many jobs as possible. If an agency form does not have a space for both prospective and current salaries, but only for the latter, then you should put down your prospective salary. You must, of course, cross out the word on the form saying 'current' salary. However, you must explain at the interview that you did this in order to be considered for a wider range of jobs; never deceive an employer about what you are now earning – they will check up.

Geographical areas Some agency forms will ask you to state only those parts of the country in which you are interested in working. Always state *all* parts of the country. You do not know, for certain, that you would not take a job in a certain area if it were offered at the right salary. In any case you want to know the kinds of jobs and salaries being offered throughout the whole country so that you can assess the job market more accurately.

Hobbies and pastimes – these are irrelevant Unless you are a school leaver leave blank the space provided for hobbies and pastimes. This information is irrelevant, can lead to personal prejudices, and in any case is none of the employer's business. If you are a school leaver see chapter 11.

Age? Rarely a barrier If your age falls outside the range specified for the job, then do not fill in your age on the form. If you can show that you can do the job, age will rarely be a barrier.

4 Writing letters

Write briefly, and except for junior jobs, by typewritten letter. Handwritten letters should be written with a fountain pen not with a ballpoint pen. Each letter must be individually composed and typed. However, do not be tempted to type your letters on your own portable typewriter. Get them typed on a good quality electric machine. If necessary, advertise in your local paper for someone to do your typing.

Never send a standard, printed or duplicated letter. Do not use paper with printed letter headings. The best paper to use is plain white, standard business size.

SETTING OUT YOUR LETTER

Be brief and to the point Head the letter with a reference to the job being advertised. For example:
Ref: Advertisement – Marketing Executive –
Daily Telegraph 13/10/77

Include only the briefest personal details of yourself. If the advertisement quotes an age range and you fall within it, and the advertisement specifically asks you to quote your age, then do so. *Otherwise never quote your age.* Age is rarely a restriction if you can subsequently prove that you can do the job. The total length of the letter should be approximately one side of standard business size paper. Anything over one and a half sides is definitely too long. Prune your draft letter until it fits into this suggested size.

The letter should be long enough to give the major areas of your experience which fit the advertisement, and any additional points which would be of special interest to a prospective employer. After reading your letter a person should be able to remember the salient points. If it is too long or too much detail is given then the picture of you is confused and the letter has to be re-read or passed over (generally the latter).

Be selective – no life histories please! Select only those items from your experience which are relevant to the particular job for which you are applying. Your main concerns should be:

> 'What experience have I which is of use to this employer and how am I going to use this experience to enable me to do this particular job?'
>
> 'How can I project myself as a positive person by quoting examples from the things which I have achieved?'
>
> 'What extra experience have I which could be of use to this employer and which could tip the scales in my favour?'

You will find later in this chapter a procedure to analyse advertisements and select those aspects of your career which meet their requirements.

Write in simple style Avoid using business jargon or hackneyed expressions. Your letter should be written in a simple style which should read naturally as if spoken. Avoid the following type of expressions:

> a life times service . . .
> welcome the opportunity . . .
> would welcome a move to . . .
> extensive experience . . .
> my current post . . .
> I feel sure that . . .
> a wealth of experience . . .
> I can truthfully say . . .

Experience of function is most important Your experience, which you will be offering an employer, will be either by function (that is doing a similar type of job) or by experience of the actual product involved. For example, for a job selling frozen foods you may have experience as a salesman or of frozen foods. Decide where your main experience for the job lies – function or product. This will be your main selling point. In general, *experience by function is the most important.* In the preceding example, it would be more important to show evidence of being a competent salesman than to show that you have an extensive knowledge of frozen foods. Similarly, for management type jobs, evidence of previous management or supervisory experience is more important than knowledge of a particular product. It is, therefore, most important in your letter of application and interview that you stress experience in the function of the job being advertised and select relevant points from your career to substantiate this.

Why are you writing the letter? No job is offered on the basis of your letter of application. *Your letter is solely to gain an interview.* Write your letter so that the employer thinks: 'We must see this person – he sounds as though he could be the person we are looking for'.

If you put too much detail in your letter, the employer can build up too detailed a picture of you and will be tempted to judge you solely on the basis of your letter – in most cases turning you down since there will always be some point to take exception to. *You must write sufficient only to whet the appetite for more.*

Application forms – never return them alone Always return an application form with a covering letter which contains your main effort in getting the prospective employer to interview you. You can put over your experience so much better in a letter. A well composed letter will always carry more weight than a form.

Analyse the advertisement – pick it to pieces When replying to an advertisement you must analyse the advertisement first to determine the specific requirements and experience required for the job. *Write down these points.* These will be points which will be specifically mentioned in the advertisement. There will also be other points which can be determined from it by thinking about the other requirements of the job, and which, although, not mentioned specifically are nevertheless necessary for doing the job. These latter points are referred to as 'hidden' qualities. In your letter of application you must draw from your experience instances to support both the specific and hidden qualities required.

Avoid giving too detailed an impression of yourself Personal details will give the person reading your letter too complete a picture of you. It will give him the temptation of rejecting you on the strength of your letter alone. You must avoid this situation, by avoiding the following points:

age
marital status
present salary
hobbies
sporting interests
religion
spare time interests

Never give your reasons for leaving your present organization. You are writing solely because you are replying to an advertisement.
If you give reasons why you want to leave your present job you may be rejected because the person reading your letter is not in sympathy with them. Do not give him this chance to reject you.

WRITING DIRECTLY

You can approach organizations with a letter even though you have seen no advertisement. These letters should be short, to the point, individually composed and written, and contain the following ingredients:

- Address the letter to a person – not a function. Ring up the organization and ask the telephone operator who the personnel manager is, etc.
- Explain briefly why you are writing.
- Project a positive image of yourself and show how you can help the particular company to which you are writing.
- Give the impression that you have singled out just this organization to apply to.

Examples of these letters are given at the end of this chapter.

Write a draft letter first – then sleep on it Never send your letter the day the advertisement appears. Write a draft letter first, then write the final version after a further two days when you have had time to think it over properly. Get your letter typed. If you follow this procedure then your letter will have a more favourable chance of being successful since:

It will be more effective because of the extra time spent on its composition.

It will arrive after the main flood of letters have been received and sifted, and will stand a better chance of being selected.

Expect to spend at least three hours composing your first draft.

Check your letter once more

re-read your typed letter for mistakes
check the address and box numbers
check that the letter is correctly headed
sign your name
fold the letter as few times as possible
check the address on the envelope
post it first class
file a copy of the letter

Note Never enclose anything else (such as specimens of work, testimonials, certificates, photographs, press cuttings, etc.) unless they are specifically requested.

EXAMPLES OF ADVERTISEMENTS AND LETTERS

Read through the following examples of advertisements, their analysis and letters of application with comments. Note that each advertisement has been analysed into requirements which are mentioned specifically and also requirements which although not mentioned specifically are nevertheless necessary for the job. Base your letters on their examples.

REPLYING TO ADVERTISEMENTS

Example 1

> Ford Main Dealer requires a clerk/typist for their Parts Department. Applicants must have accurate typing and be willing to undertake varied work. Reply to: Smith Motor Co. Ltd., 14 Innsworth Lane, Staines, Middlesex.

Specific requirements

- accurate typing
- adaptability, to undertake varied work

Hidden requirements

- ability to deal with customers, could be over the telephone dealing with customer enquiries, or occasionally at a service counter
- accuracy with figures, taking down and looking up part numbers, dealing with invoices, etc.

Letter 1A – poor

> 22 Bridge Street,
> Esher,
> Surrey.
> 14/12/77
>
> The Manager,
> Smith Motor Co. Ltd.,
> 14 Innsworth Lane,
> Staines, Middlesex.
>
> Dear Sir,
>
> I am replying for the job of clerk/typist advertised in the Weekly Post. I am at present working for Smith & Son as a typist in the General Office and have to be accurate in my work. I have worked for Smith & Son for two years. Previous to that I worked for Jones the Solicitors. At school I obtained the C.S.E. in 4 subjects and did typing training gaining the Stage II certificate. I am age 22 years, single and am at present earning £40 per week. In my spare time I support the local Church Fellowship.
>
> Yours faithfully,

Letter 1B – good

14 Long Lodge Drive,
Southall,
Middlesex.

14th December, 1977

The Manager,
Smith Motor Co. Ltd.,
14 Innsworth Lane,
Staines,
Middlesex.

Dear Sir,

Ref: Advertisement – clerk/typist

Parts Department

I am replying to your advertisement in the Weekly Post for a clerk/typist in your Parts Department.

For the past two years I have been employed by a firm of wholesalers as a typist in the General Office. This work involves not only typing, but filing, answering customers' queries by telephone and using a calculator to add up accounts.

Previous to working for my present employer I worked for a firm of solicitors. The typing of legal documents required very accurate work.

Although I enjoy typing, I am keen to undertake any office duties you may require and feel I would be able to deal with customers either by telephone or over the counter.

Yours faithfully,

A.M. Brown

Comments on Letter 1A

- too many personal details
- age should not be mentioned
- present employer should not be given
- present salary should not be given
- hobbies, sparetime, or pastimes are irrelevant

Comments on Letter 1B

- letter answers specific and hidden requirements
- prospective employer cannot get a prejudiced view of the applicant because no personal details have been given
- the person sounds hardworking and someone who can use their initiative
- the letter whets the appetite for more and generates the thought that 'we must interview this person!'

REPLYING TO ADVERTISEMENTS

Example 2

> Chief Accountant wanted for medium sized but expanding private manufacturing company. Must be experienced in management accounting and computerized accounting systems. Salary £7,000 per annum. Reply with brief details quoting ref: DR 101 to the Personnel Manager, Jack Tools, 44 Bridge Road, Westminster, London.

Specific requirements

- experience of management accounting
- experience of computerized accounting

Hidden requirements

- ability to deal with company expansion
- experience of dealing with Boards of directors as a chief Accountant would have to prepare reports and statements for his directors
- ability to participate in long term planning because the company is expanding

Letter 2A – poor

14 Church Street,
Barrymore,
Gloucester.

The Personnel Manager
Jack Tools,
44 Bridge Road,
Westminster, London.

23/4/76

Dear Sir,

I am writing in reply to your advertisement in the Daily Telegraph for a Chief Accountant.

I am 35 years of age, married with two children. My qualifications are B.Sc(Econ) and Associate Membership of the Institute of Chartered Accountants.

For the last 4 years I have been assistant to the Chief Accountant of the General Manufacturing Co., Hereford. I have special responsibilities for management accounting and use the output from a computer for drawing up the yearly budgets. My present salary is £6,500 per annum.

I believe that I am now ready to take on the responsibilities of a chief accountant since I have had experience of all aspects of accountancy and have deputized for the Chief Accountant on many occasions.

Yours faithfully,

Letter 2B – good

23 Sandridge Avenue,
Bolton,
Lancs.

The Personnel Manager,
Jack Tools,
44 Bridge Road,
Westminster,
London.

23rd April, 1976

Dear Sir,

Re: Advertisement for Chief Accountant – Daily Telegraph/DR101

I am assistant to the Chief Accountant of a manufacturing group. I have worked for this group for the last 4 years during which time it has grown from a medium size company to a large group with a turnover of £300 million per year. This development has been a result of internal growth and by the acquisition of other companies. I thus have a lot of experience of the problems caused by rapid growth.

Among my duties are those of leading the Management Accounting team, preparing yearly budgets with the aid of a computer and producing reports for consideration by the Board of Directors.

I have recently completed a study of the cash flow of my company for the next 5 years. This has taken account of many factors such as new product launches, expansion of factory space and workforce, and possible acquisition of other companies. This plan has been accepted by the Board of Directors and has been instrumental in their decision for the company to go public in the next year.

I look forward to hearing from you.

Yours faithfully,

E.R. Nicklson

Comments on Letter 2A

- too many irrelevant details about age, qualifications, etc
- present salary should not be quoted
- complete failure to analyse the advertisement for hidden requirements
- not enough substantiation of experience
- has given reason for leaving ' . . . now ready to take on responsibilities . . .'. This should not be included as the letter itself should imply this without it having to be spelt out

Comments on Letter 2B

- all specific and hidden requirements have been answered
- no personal details have been given
- present salary not mentioned
- gives an impression that the person can handle all aspects of the job
- is obviously a valuable person to have in view of his experience in company expansion and knowledge of the procedure for going public
- the letter is concise but covers all aspects of the job

REPLYING TO ADVERTISEMENTS

Example 3

> **We need**
>
> **A Young Person**
>
> (18-45) to operate our forecourt console. This is a responsible position where you need to be good at figures and have a pleasant approach to customers. Good pay and conditions with friendly atmosphere.

Specific requirements

- good at figures
- experience of dealings with customers

Hidden requirements

- ability to work on one's own initiative, as this is a responsible position
- used to handling cash
- honesty since cash is involved
- ability to get on well with colleagues as 'friendly atmosphere' implies working with other staff

Letter 3A – poor

46 Commercial Road,
Highbury,
Birmingham 8.

12/12/76

The Manager,
The Forward Garage Co. Ltd.,
65 High Street,
London S.W.8.

Dear Sir,

I am replying to your letter for a young person to operate the forecourt console. I am 18 years of age and, at present, work in a shop. I am not sure what career I want to go in for but I think I could do the job you are advertising. I would be keen to be promoted after about a year. You mention good pay and conditions, could you tell me how much you will be paying and how long the holidays are?

Yours faithfully,

Letter 3B – good

35 Ashley Park,
Newlands,
Bristol 8.
12 December, 1976

The Manager,
The Forward Garage Co. Ltd.,
65 High Street,
London S.W.8.

Dear Sir,

Ref: Advertisement – Young Person

I am replying to your advertisement for a young person to operate the forecourt console.

I am at present working in a shop, where I am dealing with customers all day. I look after one small department and am responsibile for taking the cash at the end of the day to the Manager.

I enjoy working with other people and meeting customers. I like being busy and would be pleased to do any other duties as might be appropriate.

Yours faithfully,

B.S. Weber

Comments on letter 3A

- should not have mentioned age
- shows too much interest in salary and conditions
- should not discuss possible promotion
- sounds as though this person thinks that the world owes him a living

Comments on letter 3B

- shows how responsibilities are relevant for the prospective job
- gives an impression of being a positive person
- sounds as though the person is hardworking and would be very useful to have around

REPLYING TO ADVERTISEMENTS

Example 4

> **Senior Piping Designers**
>
> Minimum qualifications HNC with 15 years experience in the oil and gas industry or related fields in order to control all drawing office functions. The salaries for all the above positions are up to £18,000 per annum net of Syrian taxes.
> Interested candidates should forward résumés and particulars including address and telephone numbers plus photocopies of education certificates.
>
> Reply to Box 1234, The Daily Telegraph.

Specific requirements

- H N C qualifications
- 15 years experience in the oil or gas industry
- experience of drawing offices
- readiness to work in Syria

Hidden requirements

- supervisory or management experience
- the job probably includes supervising less skilled staff

Letter 4A – poor

17 Newbury Road,
Newport,
Monmouth.

Box 1234,
The Daily Telegraph,
135 Fleet Street,
London E.C.4. 12/1/78

Dear Sir,

I am replying to your advertisement for a Senior Piping Designer.

I am 35 years old and have an HNC in Mechanical Engineering. At present I am employed by John Brown as a Senior Designer, and have worked for them for the last 16 years. Much of my working life has been spent drawing out piping layouts. Thus I have a wealth of experience in this field.

During my time with John Brown I have also worked as a field engineer and have had experience of other drawing office duties.

My present company has found difficulty obtaining new orders and I want to leave and join a more progressive and profitable one.

I am very keen to travel and work abroad, particularly in the Middle East and look forward to hearing from you.

Yours faithfully,

Letter 4B – good

43 Bootle Road,
Twigworth,
Oxford.
12th January, 1978

Box 1234,
The Daily Telegraph,
135 Fleet Street,
London E.C.4.

Dear Sir,

Re: Advertisement – Senior Piping Designers

I am replying to the above advertisement and believe I have the experience you are looking for since I have been working in the petro-chemicals industry for the last 16 years. At present I am a Section Leader for a small team designing oil pipe layouts.

My present job consists of designing piping layouts, supervising juniors, liaising with field and planning engineers and also producing costings for estimating purposes.

I have spent some time assisting field engineers on site and believe I have a good all round knowledge of pipe designing and erection, together with the necessary procedures required in the drawing office.

I have recently spent some time at the local technical college assisting the Engineering department in the investigation of new welding techniques being specially developed for the oil industry. These techniques give a very high quality weld with less skilled labour than is normally required.

Now that my children are grown up, I am free to work abroad and look forward to hearing from you.

Yours faithfully,

M.S.Brown

Comments on letter 4A

- has not really answered the advertisement
- should not have mentioned age
- '. . . a wealth of experience . . .' is a trite phrase
  should not give reason for wanting to leave

Comments on letter 4B

- has answered all the qualities mentioned
- gives impression of a well-experienced designer
- shows that he gets on well with people
- has initiative to learn new methods
- has special knowledge which could be very useful

REPLYING TO ADVERTISEMENTS

Example 5

> **Used Car**
> **Sales executive**
>
> to manage new modern car premises specialising in low mileage cars up to 4 years old. Candidates should be between 30/40 years of age and have several years experience in the used car field. Must be self motivated and capable of appraising, valuing and buying used cars. Remuneration by salary plus commission of generated profits, pension scheme.

Specific requirements

- experience of the used car field
- self-motivated
- ability to appraise, value and buy used cars
- management ability

Hidden requirements

- working with little direction
- profit awareness

Letter 5A – poor

14 Bath Street,
Backside,
Bristol 6.

12th August, 1977

The Managing Director,
The Clean Car Co. Ltd.,
Bishopsgate,
London W.8.

Dear Sir,

I am writing for the position of Used Car Sales Executive. I am, at present, employed with Johnson & Sons which is the main Ford dealer in South London. I am 37 years of age and my salary and commission last year was £6,500. I have been with my present company for 6 years and have progressed from junior salesman to senior salesman. I have a wealth of experience in the car trade and I believe I am now ready for a management job.

Approximately half my time is spent in going out appraising and buying secondhand cars, the rest of my time is selling and dealing with customers.

I am always suggesting new ideas but these are not often taken up, as my boss is too conservative; this is one of the reasons why I would welcome a move to a more progressive company.

I am a member of the local Round Table Association and am an active member of the local church.

I look forward to hearing from you.

Yours faithfully,

Letter 5B – good

95 Coal Road,
Berrystone,
Newcastle.

The Managing Director,
The Clean Car Co. Ltd.,
Bishopsgate,
London W.8.

12th August, 1977

Dear Sir,

Re: Advertisement: Used Car Sales Executive

I am writing in reply to your advertisement for the above position.

My present company is a large motor car agency and I have the responsibility for the used car sales. Since the company only deals with cars less than 5 years old, I am responsible for selecting good quality used cars either from our customers or trade sources.

I have a staff of two salesmen, a junior and a clerk/typist. My department is considered as a profit centre and, as such, is charged for overheads, servicing and preparation of the used cars before sale. I have been able to increase the profit of the department each year, not only in absolute terms but also as a percentage of turnover.

Although my present employer is very conservative in nature, I have been able to make several suggestions which have increased our share of the local used car market.

I have also been able to build up my experience of the servicing and accounts side of the business. I now have good all round practical experience of running a used car business.

I look forward to hearing from you,

Yours faithfully,

E.S. Made

Comments on letter 5A

- age and salary should not be quoted
- irrelevant details about hobbies and interests should not be quoted
- prospective employers are not interested in whether you believe you are ready for management, *you must demonstrate it.* This is also used as a reason for leaving should not criticize present employer
- '. . . would welcome a move to . . .' is a trite phrase

Comments on letter 5B

- management ability has been stressed
- profitability has been demonstrated
- shows that the candidate is aware of all aspects of running a used car business
- this person obviously has ideas which would be of benefit to a prospective employer

DIRECT LETTERS

The following letters illustrate examples of writing directly without any advertisement appearing. In all three cases the organisations concerned could well be thinking of employing someone in the respective positions and could be taking steps to place advertisements in the near future. If the writers of these letters proved acceptable they would almost certainly be hired and the proposed advertisements cancelled.

DIRECT LETTER

Example 1

95 Blythe Road,
Hounslow,
Middlesex.

Mr. R.A. Dixon,
Sales Manager,
Norwood Actuators Ltd.,
Selkirk,
Manchester 6.

12th April, 1976

Dear Sir,

I am writing to you because I would like you to consider me for a position in your sales staff.

I have noted from advertisements in the press that you are taking on more office staff and thought it likely that you would be interested in extra sales staff as well.

For the last five years I have worked for a large multinational company selling electronic actuators. The products which I currently sell overlap your company's products in some areas of the market, so I am accustomed to the type of companies which you trade with. I am particularly interested in your new range of actuators and have several ideas for making improvements to them.

I have reached my sales quota every year for the last three years and if I joined your company I believe I could have a beneficial influence on the design of the products themselves as well as selling them.

If you have a suitable vacancy I look forward to hearing from you.

Yours faithfully,

A.J. Robertson

DIRECT LETTER

Example 2

46 Clive Road,
Acton,
Middlesex.
12/4/77

Mr. F.S. Cooper,
The Personnel Manager,
Glums Department Store,
London Road,
Gloucester.

Dear Sir,

I am moving to the Gloucester area in the next year and would appreciate if you could consider me for a position in your Department Store.

For the last eight years I have been employed by one of the main stores in Kingston-On-Thames. I work in the Hardware and Electrical Department and am responsible for a section selling household domestic appliances. I work directly for the buyer and would have planned to take over his job when he retires in two years times. At the moment, I stand in for him when he is away.

My department has been very successful in boosting off-season sales by special offers and extended guarantees and by several suggestions of mine which have proved successful.

I have visited your store when I have stayed in Gloucester and have found the staff extremely pleasant and helpful. I am sure that I could fit in well and would prove a hardworking and loyal member of your staff.

Yours faithfully,

G.R. Evans

DIRECT LETTER

Example 3

22 Glen Close,
Oxford,
Oxon.
24th April, 1978

Mr. G.A. Holt,
The Managing Director,
Ajax Electronic Equipment Ltd.,
Slough Road,
Swindon.

Dear Sir,

I am a specialist in market research in the area of electronics recording instruments. At the moment I am part of a small team in a large company which have found this very valuable for predicting the suitability of its products for the market.

A growing number of medium size companies now find it worth their while to have at least one person doing this function. As you are aware, the competition from foreign suppliers is very intense, but by judiciously selecting the areas of the market to aim at, much unproductive and wasteful effort can be eliminated. My present company has managed to produce and sell equipment which fills particular requirements not covered by competitive suppliers. The sale of this specialized equipment also brings in orders for the more popular types as well.

If you are thinking of providing such a market research function in your company, I would be glad to come and talk about it with a view to joining your firm and providing a market research service for you.

Yours faithfully,

A.J. Roberts

CHECKLIST FOR APPLICATION LETTERS

Complete the points below:

1) Analyse the advertisement for specific and hidden qualities.

Specific requirements 1 . . . .
2 . . . .
3 . . . .
4 . . . .

Hidden requirements 1 . . . .
2 . . . .
3 . . . .
4 . . . .

2) Draft letter written?

3) Checked advertisement and reference numbers?

4) Checked address/box number?

5) Left out personal details?

6) Left out clichés or hackneyed phrases?

7) Left out reasons for leaving present employer?

8) Final letter typed?

9) Used plain paper?

10) White standard, business size paper used?

11) Re-read letter for mistakes?

12) Letter signed?

13) Minimum number of folds?

14) Posted First Class at least four days after advertisement appeared?

5 Preparation for the interview

If you are offered an interview, first write back thanking the company for the offer of interview and confirm the date, place and time of interview. This letter should also be typewritten. When the interviewer reviews your correspondence at the interview, the sight of well set out typewritten letters will greatly impress him.

STUDYING THE ORGANIZATION

Study the prospective employer well Get as much information as possible about your prospective employer. An interviewee who has this information and shows that he knows thoroughly about the interviewer's company has an advantage over other candidates. Go to a business library and read up about the company. Study their annual reports. Although you will probably never use 95 per cent of the information you glean – the added confidence which this knowledge gives you will definitely show up at the interview. Even one single comment which shows that you know and understand the company, could land you the job.

How is the company constituted? If the prospective employer is a company, is it a private or public company? Is it a subsidiary of another company? Who ultimately owns it? At one extreme the owner will be the person who actually runs the company. At the other extreme the company, which you will be joining, could be one small unit in a vast international operation (although this may not be apparent at the time). For example:

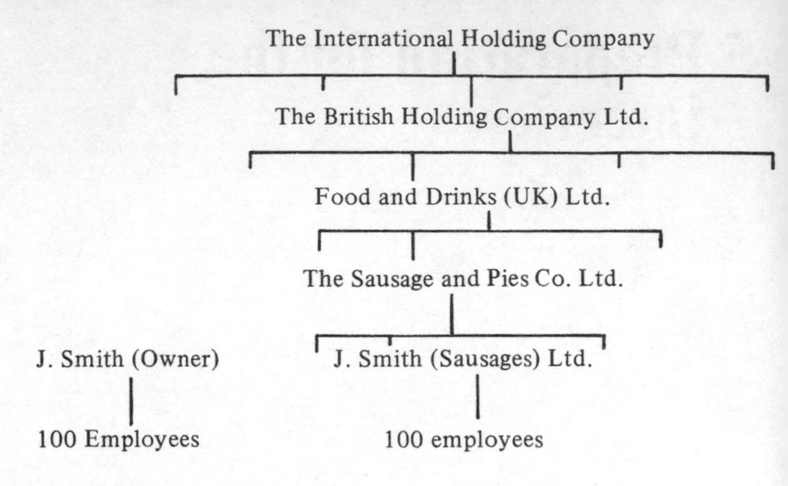

The interviewer will doubtless explain the constitution of the company at the interview, and if you interject suitable comments which show that you know about his company this is bound to impress him. Even though you do not get a chance to show your knowledge at the interview, the fact that you have it, will boost your confidence. Underlying knowledge, even though never used, always promotes confidence.

What are the company's products? Find out about the company's products, and also the competition's products. What are their weaknesses? You could ask a competitor for his comments. Go to your local library and read up the back number copies of the appropriate trade journals to get good background knowledge of the market in which the company operates.

You can use the knowledge, which you have gained, to good effect, at the interview, by asking penetrating questions about the firm's product range and plans for future development. This gets the message over to the interviewer that you are really interested in the job and organized to get it.

Get plenty of literature Ring up the company and ask for all the relevant literature which they can let you have. Collect it yourself if necessary. *Then read it*. Useful literature to obtain:

product brochures
annual financial statements
chairman's reports
illustrated catalogues and price lists

On the day before the interview read this literature again.

Intelligence tests – be prepared! Interviews are sometimes preceded by tests of various sorts. There are three categories of tests:

1) Intelligence tests. These take about one hour to complete and are usually split into three sub-tests as follows:

a) Measurement of powers of perception or logical reasoning using diagrams, sequences of letters or numbers, etc. HINT if you are required to manipulate letters of the alphabet, write the alphabet down on a scrap of paper and underneath the letters write their corresponding numbers. You will find that manipulating numbers is easier.

b) Literary ability using words or phrases. This is to find out your comprehension of the language.

c) Numeracy – manipulating numbers, doing mental arithmetic, etc.

2) Trade tests. Where some manipulative ability is required these tests can rule out candidates who, while they may have the intelligence to learn a manipulative process, must be rejected, because they lack the dexterity to achieve economic rates of output. These tests are usually required for jobs requiring craftmanship and physical skill.

3) Psychological tests. These are of a specialized nature and have as their objective, the gaining of insight into the character and behaviour of the candidate.

No one is hired as the result of their achievement in a test. The results of tests are used to complement the candidate's performance at interview. Two specific uses for tests are:

1) To provide a cut-off in that candidates with a score less than an acceptable minimum will not be hired no matter how good their other attributes. For example a computer programmer must score above a minimum in logical reasoning tests even before he is accepted for interview.

2) To compare the results of a candidate with the results of typical people already doing similar jobs.

It is recommended that you buy a book of intelligence tests and work through them in the week before the interview. This will enable you to give of your best and not spend valuable time or wasted points learning how to do them at the interview. Do not be tempted to guess answers to questions as marks are usually subtracted for wrong answers. Thus, if you guess you will not increase your score but with more answers wrong you will detract from your performance.

Graphology (handwriting analysis) There is an increasing use of graphology by companies in an attempt to analyse the character and abilities of candidates. The uses of graphology can be split into two areas:

1) A general character analysis of the individual.

2) The grading of candidates according to specific abilities which are required for the job in question.

For example an employer filling a vacancy for a salesman may require that candidates be graded according to their score in the following abilities:

tenacity of purpose
extroversion
ability to work with others

The use of graphology can analyse a person in the following four areas for the specific qualities listed under each area.

a) Temperament:

self reliance
serenity
excitability
nervousness
phlegm

b) Mental and intellectual qualities:

intelligence
perception
memory
observation
judgement
logical reasoning

c) Social tendencies:

extroversion/introversion
tenacity of purpose
concentration
ability to work with others

d) Moral qualities:

generosity
selfishness
spite
jealousy

The graphologist prefers material written with an ink rather than a ball point pen. This is because an ink pen is able to show variations in the pressure of the strokes and this enables a more complete analysis to be performed. You will invariably be asked for an existing specimen of your handwriting rather than being asked to produce a specimen at the interview (which could be unrepresentative due to the stressful situation). If, however, you are asked to produce a specimen of handwriting you should observe the following rules.

1) Use an ink pen.

2) Write your specimen when you are feeling alert, calm and fresh, not when you are feeling tired and anxious.

3) Write as naturally as possible in your own style but be as neat as possible within that style.

Build yourself up – 'the power of positive thinking' For the week before the interview, think of yourself in the position applied for. Build yourself up to the job you are asking for and are determined to get. Think of the problems of the job and how you would tackle them. Try and live the job for the week before the interview.

Public speaking – rehearse Some interviews are preceded by group interviews of all the candidates together. During this time it is probable that you will have to address the audience by standing up and speaking to them. Rehearse your public speaking as described in the chapter on group interviews. Try to be first; you will then be noticed as a positive person and because you will have rehearsed your talk, will be difficult for the others to live up to.

Be interviewed last! You stand a better chance. When your letter arrives requesting you to attend for interview, ring the secretary of the person arranging the interview and sound her out about interview times. Try to be the last person to be interviewed. Failing that be first. Get your interview time changed if necessary.

You should be last because the interviewer needs several sessions to settle into the interview and lose his self-consciousness. If you are the last person to be interviewed and give a good account of yourself you will leave him with a stronger impression than the other candidates. If you fail to be last then try to be first. Your interview will then be a model which the others have to live up to.

Agencies – no recommendations please If you are one of a number of candidates being sent along to the interview by an agency or consultant instruct them not to recommend you in preference to other candidates. Being so recommended will diminish your chances of getting the job. The interviewer will be expecting too high a standard of you, and will pick some other candidate for the job just to show the consultant that he has an independent opinion.

Brief wife/husband – be good at public relations! Brief your wife or husband on answering the telephone in your absence. Leave your diary by the telephone so that an interview can be arranged or changed in your absence. A business-like and efficient spouse is a credit to you. The impression which you give to an employer over the telephone, especially to his secretary, adds up to the overall picture which he is building up of you. Do you and your spouse give a picture of efficiency and competence over the telephone? *Rehearse and* *know in advance* what you will both say. Let your wife know where you can be contacted during the day so that interview times can be confirmed quickly and efficiently.

File your references, specimens, etc. Be business-like. Put your previous references, if available, neatly filed in a *new* file. This can also contain specimens of work – drawings, reports, proposals, letters, etc. The first item in the file should be an index of its contents. This file can be taken along to the interview and the necessary specimens produced on the spot.

It should be left with the secretary of the interviewer prior to the interview. If needed the interviewer can call his secretary for it to be brought in. This creates a good business-like impression, and is better than you taking the file in to the interview with you and not knowing what to do with it or where to put it.

Personal appearances – they do count! Appearances do count. The interviewer has never seen you before and first impressions are important. The following are some good tips:

- Have your hair cut at least five days before the interview, or not at all. If you have your hair cut immediately before an interview it is too obvious that you have smartened up especially for the interview, and this detracts from the overall impression of you, since it implies that you are not usually smart.
- Have your clothes cleaned and pressed.
- Men! Wear a new shirt and new tie.
- Make sure that your shoes have been cleaned and do not need repairing.
- For men, long socks, pulled up, are definitely more business-like than ankle-length socks.
- If your glasses are old and discoloured, why not get a new pair in the latest fashion.
- Get rid of raincoats or overcoats. Give them to the secretary before going into the interview.
- Ladies! Sort your handbag out *before* the interview.

Dress smartly: we all know it's a special occasion but at least it shows that you can make an effort, some people can't even do that!

Get there on time! Make sure that you can get to the interview on time. If going by car add at least half an hour to the normal journey time to allow for traffic hold-ups, punctures, etc. If you are going by public transport be pessimistic about making connections at railway stations, etc.

If you have not been to the address of the interview before, make a trial run a few days before the interview. Should you arrive late you will also arrive hot, bothered and dishevelled and will start off by making apologies for yourself. You will never recover your composure. If you cannot organize yourself to get to an important event, like a job interview, on time then you do not deserve to be considered for the job at all.

The power of positive thinking – it works When you arrive at the place of interview, take ten minutes walking slowly around the block to compose yourself and build yourself up into the right mental attitude for the interview. Say to yourself:

> I *am* going to give a good interview
> I am *just* the person they want
> I feel *great*
> This is just the job for *me*
> I have done my homework and *I feel terrific*

THE MEMORY FORMULA

Before writing your letter of application, you will have analysed the advertisement for the specific and hidden requirements for the job. Write these requirements down again. Now write specific examples taken from your own experience to support each of these requirements. These requirements and examples MUST BE MEMORIZED so that they can be produced at interview and discussed in detail. To avoid forgetting them at the interview write them on a card and take it with you. Study the following examples.

ANALYSING ADVERTISEMENTS

Example 1

Personal Assistant To Service Manager

Invoice typist to process all incoming orders and generally help with different duties within the Service Department.

Salary negotiable.

Requirement varied typing experience
My example **1** Typing of invoices which is approximately 30

per cent of the work.
2 Typing of confidential letters for the Credit and Service Managers.
3 Typing of reports.

Requirement good adaptibility
My example 1 Helping with filing.
2 Occasionally dealing with customer queries.
3 Have helped with stock audits.

Requirement experience as a personal assistant
My example 1 Occasionally deputizing for present manager.
2 Supervising the Post Room.

ANALYSING ADVERTISEMENTS
Example 2

> **Infra-red Engineer**
>
> Required by leading manufacturers of industrial process heating equipment located in Bletchley, Bucks, to be involved in estimating, design and customer liaison.
> Applicants should have experience in this field, especially on gas fired equipment.
> Rented housing available.

Requirement experience of infra-red equipment
My example 1 Have designed infra-red equipment for 3 years.
2 Have responsibility for one junior designer.

Requirement experience of estimating
My example 1 Have worked closely with estimators to produce designs of least cost.
2 Have estimated two pieces of equipment.

Requirement experience of customer liaison
My example 1 Dealings with customers by telephone.
2 Experience of customer site work.

Requirement production of technical reports
My example 1 Have written a technical manual.
2 Have produced a feasibility report.

ANALYSING ADVERTISEMENTS
Example 3

> **Personnel Officer**
>
> An opportunity has arisen for a young graduate (male or female) with some formal training in Personnel Management.
> Reporting to the Personnel Manager the successful applicant will cover a wide range of personnel duties including recruitment, communications, legislation and administration.
> Salary will be negotiable, according to experience, with good career prospects to be expected from a major Company.

Requirement formal training in Personnel Management
My example 1 Have attended evening classes in Personnel Management.
2 Have passed professional examinations.

Requirement experience in Personnel Management
My example 1 Have deputized for the Personnel Manager.
2 Responsible for looking at new legislation.
3 Have prepared reports on Personnel policy for the directors.

Requirement experience of salary negotiations
My example 1 Have negotiated pay settlements with the Electrical Trade Union.
2 Have helped review the salary structure in my present company.

ANALYSING ADVERTISEMENTS
Example 4

> **Sales Engineers**
>
> **in several areas including**
> **London, Home Counties & North of England**
> We are a successful and fast expanding private Company in Electronic Component distribution and are seeking to expand our field Sales force.
> Preference will be given to dynamic people who are self motivated and keen to advance within the Company.
> Candidates should be aged between 24-35 and have some engineering qualifications.

Requirement experience of selling
My example 1 3 years with present company.
2 4 years with a previous company.

Requirement dynamic and self motivated
My example 1 Organized special sales promotion week.
2 Have run technical courses for other salesmen.

Requirement management potential
My example 1 Supervision of trainee salesmen.
2 Have taken a business studies course.

Requirement engineering qualifications
My example 1 ONC in engineering.

CHECKLIST FOR PREPARATION FOR THE INTERVIEW

Complete each of the points below as they are accomplished

Confirmed date, place, time of interview?

Obtained information on the company and read it?

Completed intelligence test training?

Rehearsed speeches?

Briefed spouse on answering telephone?

Written down examples of experience and memorized?

Collected references, specimens, etc. and filed in new folder with index?

Trial run to interview address?

Hair cut?

Suit cleaned and pressed?

New shirt and tie?

6 What the interviewer is looking for

The interviewer has two methods of judging your suitability for the job:

1) By questioning you and evaluating the things about you and your experience which you tell him. This procedure is discussed in the following sections of this chapter.
2) By observing how you handle the interview itself.

If you have obviously planned your interview well, by showing that you are knowledgeable about the organization and by asking penetrating questions, then the interviewer will assume that you are also capable of planning and making a good job of your work. The converse is also true – a bad performance at interview could (but not necessarily) mean an unsatisfactory performance at the job.

If you have the experience and ability to do the job then make sure that you do not let your interview performance let you down. Since in almost all cases, the interviewer has no prior knowledge of the candidates (except their letter of application) he will make up his mind on who to employ solely on his assessment of each one at interview. Even if all candidates *could* do the job equally well, some will give the impression that they will do better than others, and some will give the impression that they are extremely unsuitable. It is up to you which impression *you* give.

The interviewer is judging you on five main areas of your life. The relative importance attached to each one can be seen from the figure opposite.

If you are of only average intelligence, have few qualifications, do not make a big impact on others and are not particularly well-adjusted – do not despair. The most important factor is *your actual achievements* and the *positive* way in which you put these over to the interviewer.

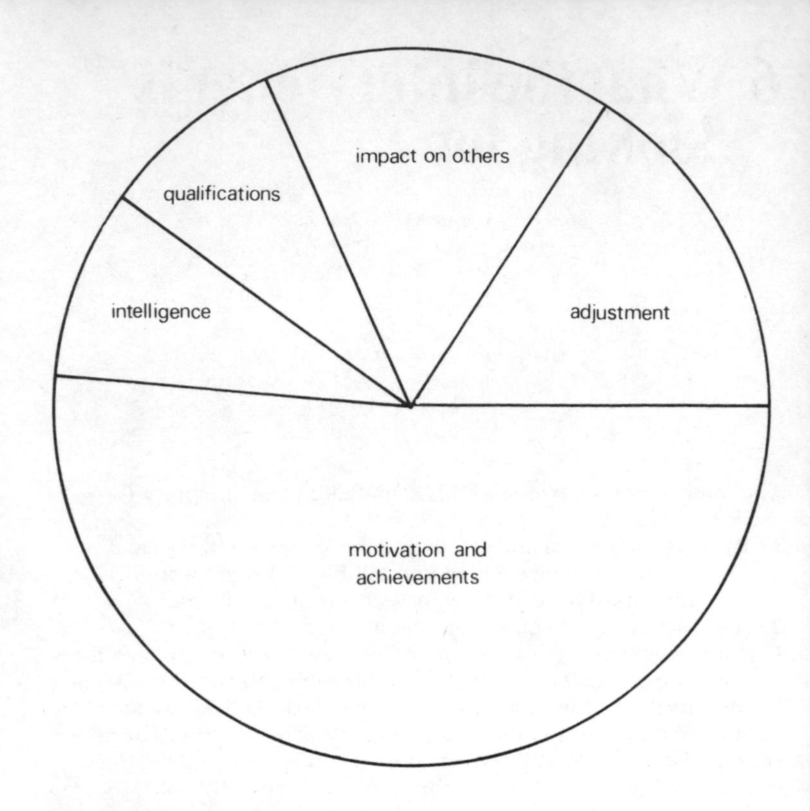

INTELLIGENCE

How do you rate for the job which you have to do? What are your cognitive powers to take in and interpret information? Are you quick at learning and what intellectual capacity have you for absorbing training?

- dull – need questions repeated or rephrased
- **quick – simple and concise answers to questions***
- too intelligent – gives complicated answers to simple questions – maybe too much of a thinker and not a doer!

***Desirable**

QUALIFICATIONS

Do you have the basic qualifications necessary for the particular job? What are your achievements at: school, university and extra-mural studies?

- If you have few formal qualifications, have you, by your own efforts, brought yourself up to the required standard?

- Do you belong to the relevant professional institution in your field of work?
- Do you regularly read the appropriate trade journals?

IMPACT ON OTHERS

How do you speak?

- **plain English easily understood and accepted by everyone***
- dialect – can you always be understood?
- affected accent – will you annoy others?

  ***Desirable**

How do you express yourself?

- Talk in generalities – not candid or down to earth
- **Talk from experience using real life situations***
- Talk in abstracts – are you a dreamer not a doer?

  ***Desirable**

Confidence?

- reserved throughout the whole interview
- **reserved at first only, then open and candid***
- very confident the whole time – may be too cocky or covering up for lack of confidence

  ***Desirable**

Appearance?

- scruffy – for some jobs this does not matter
- average, slight slouch – not noticeable in crowd
- **well groomed, physically fit, stand up straight***
- over dressed – do you think more about your appearance than doing the job?

  ***Desirable**

ADJUSTMENT

How are you adjusted to life in general and the work about you? What is your emotional stability and how well do you control the situations which you find yourself in? Havc you a good capacity to withstand stress? What relationship do you have with other people, particularly your colleagues?

Disposition

- **sanguine – you are confident, do things on your own initiative, take some risks***
- phlegmatic – you are sluggish, need leading but pay attention to detail
- choleric – you are prickly, take things too personally, get upset easily
- melancholic – you are cheerless, lethargic and tend to brood

  ***Desirable**

Concentrate on the desirable attributes which you have!

Interests

- educational
- hobbies
- sports – are these team events?
- social/community – fund raising, charitable, etc

Do your interests reflect your social and financial situation? Are they true interests or 'the expected thing to do?' A person's interests can reflect his general health and energy levels.

Circumstances

- single/married/divorced/widowed?
- children?
- mobility?

Why are you changing your job? Can you break away from your present environment and will this cause problems for your family?

Maturity. Do you:

Negative:

- react against authority?
- blame others for your failures?
- make excessive claims for your abilities?
- depend on others for praise?
- withdraw from difficult situations?
- make promises you won't keep?

Positive:

- take your career seriously?
- take your family responsibilities seriously?
- have the ability to persevere?
- compromise?
- react constructively to criticism?

Attitudes and environment. Do you:

- think in terms of people or things?
- like repetitive work?
- talk too much?
- get easily bored?
- like company?

Are you:

- tactful?
- aggressive?
- critical?
- indifferent to others?

MOTIVATION AND ACHIEVEMENT

Apart from achievements which are relevant to the specific job, the interviewer has to assess more general attitudes which you have to achievement and work.

- Can you motivate yourself and work on your own initiative?
- Do you set yourself goals and achievements?

- Can you get things done even when faced with difficulties?
- Are your achievements above average for your age and position?
- Are you a dreamer?
- Have you long term personal goals?
- Does what you say about your career add up?
- Are you telling the truth?
- Have you reached the level one would expect for your qualifications and background?
- Where are you on your career cycle – going up, down or static?
- Which kind of work has given you the most satisfaction?
- Are you a person who can deliver on time?

The in-tray syndrome Do you spend too long working through your in-tray, producing an out-tray for someone else to work through? Many people (especially managers and supervisors) forget that their role is to:

plan goals to be achieved
direct themselves and others in the execution of these plans
control and review results
manage their own and their subordinates' time effectively

Dealing with correspondence via the in-tray and out-tray is merely a daily precursor for doing the job. All successful people understand that their day starts when they have emptied the in-tray – do you?

Are you an action driven person? The interviewer is trying to select a person who is a *doer,* an *action person* from the *dawdler, ditherer* and *incompetent.* The latter are often expert at camouflaging their inaction by eloquently propounding the many things they are always about to do, or by finding excuses for the things which they did not do.

Do you present your boss with problems or solutions? When you meet problems do you go to your boss for help? Or do you analyse the problem and define a solution or choice of solutions to present to him? If not, start now by always having one possible solution to any problem you need help with.

Do you have initiative? Do you suggest new things to be done? Do you act without being asked? Have you the confidence to trust your own judgement and act? Having initiative means taking chances – and sometimes failing.

Do you pay attention to detail? Do you resent detail – preferring to deal with 'the big picture' or 'the broad brush approach', leaving others to work out the detail? A job well done nearly always depends on attention to detail at a high level.

Do you finish the job? Many people are good starters but poor finishers. Think back over the past year. How many jobs have you started but not finished? Get into the habit of finishing off, tidying up and coming to a definite conclusion.

Can you meet deadlines? Do you work only at a single pace, or can you work faster to meet a deadline? Do you panic at deadlines? Nothing impresses more than the ability to complete a job on time. Have you got into the habit of working regular overtime, leaving yourself no slack to deal with unforeseen overloads or panic situations?

Do you perform well when the going gets tough? It is very difficult to judge people under normal conditions. However, when the going gets tough, people get a chance to show what they are really made of. When things get really tough do you:

make excuses?
pass the job onto a colleague?
fall ill?

Or do you stick the job out no matter what?

If you cannot be *positive* about the above points start now in your present job. Turn over a new leaf! Prepare for your next job by positive action now.

Are you telling the truth? Obviously the interviewer must know whether what you are saying adds up. He will try and cross check what you are saying. There is only one way to prevent yourself being caught out, *tell the truth*. In addition there are certain faults which people exhibit at interviews which can mask the real person which the interviewer is trying to find out about. The interviewer may be especially looking for evidence of these traits. Being aware of them will help prevent you displaying them. The four following points are examples of this.

Rationalization You may find yourself justifying actions or explaining situations unfavourable to you by rationalizing them, i.e. finding excuses. In this way you can hide the truth from the interviewer or even from yourself. For example you may rationalize a failed promotion by saying that the boss has favourites whereas the truth is that your work quality or quantity was not good enough.

Reaction You may express motives opposite to those which you really possess. You may say that you want a job change, because although you find your present job interesting you want more of a challenge. In fact it may be because you hate your present job and think that anything would be better than your present situation.

Projection Ascribing our own behaviour, attitudes or motives to others may be an easy and safe way of getting our own opinions over to the interviewer. For example 'The people in my department think that the manager is too old fashioned' may be a safe way of saying 'I think my boss is a fuddy-duddy'.

Identification Taking the good qualities of others as one's own especially when we are in close contact with the other people or person. 'I am very well organized' could really mean 'My boss has organized the department so well that even I appear well organized!

CHECKLIST OF POINTS WHICH IMPRESS

simple answers to questions
record of personal development
good standard English spoken
examples given from experience
not too reserved or too cocky
well groomed
confident in nature
presents solutions to problems
pays attention to detail
always finishes the job
meets deadlines
works well under pressure
has a good grasp of the facts
has initiative
isolates the important detail

Doing not dreaming

7 The interview

The job will be offered largely on your performance at the interview and *on your own assessment of yourself.* The interviewer will be using your own assessment of yourself to arrive at his assessment. After all, you have known yourself longer than he has. Hence the importance of building your confidence up before the interview.
Build your confidence by:

- doing your homework on the company
- thoroughly analysing the requirements of the job and memorizing your examples for fulfilling them
- planning the questions which you will ask

A candidate is successful because he *has convinced the interviewer that he is capable of doing the job and will do it better than any of the other candidates!*
There are two aspects to this process:

1) He has selected key items from his experience which show that he could do the job.

and more importantly

2) He has *projected himself into the job* by asking the right questions and convincing the interviewer that he knows or can work out the real problems of the job, together with their solutions. The way the candidate handles the interview itself has an effect on the interviewer's judgement in this matter.

Remember that the interviewer's job is to find a suitable applicant to fill the job. Contrary to what you may think, the interviewer is not trying to trick or trap you. He is trying to convince himself that you are the person for the job. You have to help him. He will be relieved when you do convince him that he has found the person which he is after.

HOW TO BEHAVE

Meet as equals – command respect You and the interviewer meet as equals. Do not suffer any indignities: if you have any indignities thrust upon you get up and walk out. For example if the interviewer says: 'Oh, I see your father is a semi-skilled mechanic – we generally like our people to come from a professional background!'

Get up and walk out

You will gain in confidence and your next interview will be that much better. Chances are, that the interviewer will apologise as you walk out through the door. You then have the choice of going back – *don't*.

Do not try to be pleasant – be business-like! Do not worry about having a pleasant interview. You do not need to go out of your way to find common ground such as a sporting interest, between the interviewer and yourself. You have a number of points to make, questions to ask and a plan to work to. Just get on with it.

Help the interviewer – he may need it! Many people forget that the interviewer will probably be just as nervous as you. He may be quite inexperienced at interviewing, which he may do only once or twice a year. He will welcome your speaking up during breaks in the conversation, but do not interrupt him. You must have a plan of which questions to ask and how you are going to put over your examples of the requirements of the job. If the interviewer is incapable of controlling the interview, e.g., you find that you are just talking about things which are trivial, then you have to control it. Your plan will enable you to do so.

Panel interviews – give them all a fair share You may be interviewed by a panel of people. Make sure that you look at all members of the panel equally. More points about these interviews are contained in chapter 8.

Entering the interview room – make a good impression As you are shown into the interview room, thank the person who has shown you in. Smile, take your time in walking over to the chair, and say in a firm voice, 'Good morning Sir/Gentlemen'. Do not shake hands or deposit clothes or sit down until asked to do so.

If you enter the room on your own, close the door behind you with one hand without turning your back to the interviewer. Practise this technique before the interview'

How to sit – keep your distance – but not too much Do not sit facing the interviewer directly. Pull the chair to an angle and sit about three feet from the interviewer's desk. Never touch or lean on the interviewer's table or desk. Sit back and relax. Let the interviewer do the initial talking.

Practise the above points beforehand. It is crucial that your first impressions are good. *The majority of candidates are rejected during the first minute of the interview.*

Do not be personal Do not talk about personal details, or about one's own personal likes or dislikes. This can set up prejudices with the interviewer. If this starts to happen, get the interview back to the details of the job. Everyone likes to think that their judgement is not affected by their own prejudices – but of course they are. There is no point in setting up prejudices unnecessarily, e.g., by arguing about sport, politics, cars, etc.

General do's and don'ts

do not criticize your present employer
do not smoke even if invited to do so
do not swear – even mildly
do not interrupt
do not 'interview' the interviewer
do not argue
do look at the interviewer
do smile
do always tell the truth
do use the interviewer's name
do dress conservatively

ALL THE RIGHT ANSWERS

Always say yes Always say YES to any question relating to whether you have had the relevant experience. Extract points from your experience to enable you to say yes. If, for example, you are applying for a management job and may think you do not have the right experience and the interviewer asks you if you have management experience. – Say *yes*, and add such points as 'I had to co-ordinate the efforts of several people for a project this year', or 'I have to manage my own time very carefully as I work without seeing my superior often', or 'I have to look after the trainees'. The point is – all people have experience of managing something and all people have some sort of experience of doing nearly everything *if only they will extract the relevant items from their experience.* You will almost certainly have some experience for the job for which you are applying, even if it is a career change for you.

Expand your replies – no snappy answers! Always expand your answers to avoid saying yes, no, or other single words. For example to the question, 'where did your father work?' To say 'Manchester, then Bristol', is too brief. The answer should be expanded as follows – 'He started in Manchester with an engineering firm which started off small but then expanded and took over two other companies. He was then transferred to one of these companies to set up a small machine shop – That is why we now live in Bristol'.

Reasons for leaving must be acceptable If you are asked about your reasons for leaving your present company, you must give an acceptable answer but not be drawn into a long discussion on it. Acceptable reasons for leaving are:

underpaid for the job
no security
working conditions unreasonable
want to make more progress
want to change your type of job
present employer not keeping up-to-date
the company is moving to a new location
want to be near elderly parents
want to take advantage of better schools
want more scope for harder work
too much commuting in present job
present job not challenging enough

Non-acceptable reasons for leaving are:

have to work evenings or weekends
job interferes with hobbies or sports
have been passed over for promotion
superior does not know his job
do not get on with colleagues
subordinates are idiots
top management are idiots
fancy a change
want to take life easier

Redundant – never Never say that you were redundant. After all your previous job may have been but you are definitely not. Say 'My employer was in trouble so I left'. If you are in these circumstances it is important to do some freelance work to prove that it was your previous *job* which was redundant and not *you*.

Your 'weak' points – a trick question If asked about your weak points, answer in general terms and shrug off the question, with a reply which still shows you in a good light, such as 'I suppose that I am too punctual for appointments and get annoyed with people who are not'.

This is a trick question and only a naive interviewer expects an honest answer. His job is to find out your weak points by asking you questions about your experience and career to date. If he persists in following this line of questioning, just 'stonewall' him until he gives up. Never seriously discuss any weak points which you may have.

Your 'strong points' – be ready! If asked about your strong points have an answer ready which is relevant to this specific job, such as 'I get on well with people', or 'I work well on my own initiative'.

Leave salary until you have got the job One of the golden rules of selling is: *Never discuss the price of the goods until you have sold the customer on their benefits.* Therefore, never discuss salary until you are sure that you have a good chance of being offered the job. If asked, say that you prefer to leave the topic until later. You must leave all discussion of salary until you are sure that the company want to employ you. This tactic will put you in a very strong negotiating position when the time comes. The same rules apply to holidays and perks.

Referees – by Christian name Do not give the names of referees until requested. Then give the referees' names using their Christian name. This indicates that you have a good relationship with them. A job is awarded before referees are consulted, and they will not affect the situation unless they say something very detrimental to you.

You must remember to ask the permission of referees before you give their name and to let them know when their reference is required. Check that they are not going away just when you need them.

ALL THE RIGHT QUESTIONS

Future promotion – a 'delicate question' You must ask whether the organization would expect to promote you in the next five years. This is very important. Most employers want to take on someone who will be suitable for later promotion. However, play this point very carefully and do not press it hard. Do not give the impression that you will be looking for promotion after being in the job a short time. Prospective employers do not like 'pyramid climbers' – if you are that good then why aren't you after a better job now? *Give only a hint* that you are interested in later promotion and convince the interviewer that you will make a success of the job for which you are applying.

What is expected in your first year? Find out what will be expected from you in the first year. Are you expected to re-organize a department, increase profits, sell to new customers, etc. It may be that the organization has not really thought about what specifically you will be doing. Joining this employer could be a costly mistake!

Will your first job be to clear up the mess left by someone else? Senior people should ask the following specific questions:

What important decisions will I have to make in the first six months?
What major decisions already taken will I have to implement?

If the interviewer does not know the answers to these questions, then request that he supplies them in due course.

How will your performance be measured? Find out how your performance is measured and if pay is linked to it. Will you have an annual appraisal interview? Will your performance be measured by gross sales, profit, faster turnover of stock, fewer customer complaints, etc? Will you be measured on achieving objectives which you have helped set? Ask the interviewer about the specific objectives of the job.

Last incumbent – what happened to him? Ask what happened to the last incumbent and how long he was in the job. If only a short time, then inquire about the previous incumbent to him. Some organizations have a definite policy of hiring and firing certain of their people every two years or so. Certain jobs are 'hot seats', and so it is very difficult to perform adequately in them because the lines of responsibility are too ill defined or because of pressure of work.

If the previous incumbent left to join another organization find out what he is now doing and for whom he is now working. He may be in hospital with a nervous breakdown! If the last incumbent has been moved to another office, will you also be moved after a time? Maybe fine for you – but what about your family?

Organization structure – where do I fit? Find out where you will fit into the organization. Have the interviewer draw out the relevant part of the organization on a piece of paper. As he does this, discuss with him how you will interface with your potential colleagues. This is a good time to ask about the people who you will be working with. 'Dotted line' responsibilities can be very difficult to work. You need to know:

who your manager is
who reports to you
who is at the same level as you
who you primarily deal with

Silence by the interviewer If you are suddenly aware of yourself talking, or the interviewer is looking you up and down while you are talking, interrupt yourself and get on to another subject by asking a question of the interviewer.

Requirements of the job and your examples Get over your examples from your experience of how you meet the requirements for the job. This should preferably be done in answer to questions. However, during lulls in the conversation you can introduce your points. At the end of the interview put over any remaining points.

What are the problems of the job? Ask the interviewer what he thinks are the main problems of the job, and make suitable comments taken from your experience in meeting these problems. This is another chance to put over your examples of how you meet the requirements of the job. Typical problem areas are:

- understanding complicated technical products
- co-ordinating the efforts of people not directly reporting to you
- managing specialists
- satisfying rapidly changing markets
- handling constantly changing technical specifications
- working to other people's plans and commitments
- motivating people in low paid or boring jobs
- not knowing what is expected of you
- handling 'political' situations
- working within unrealistic or constantly changing budgets

Show your knowledge of the organization – but do not boast Show that you know about the organization and its products or services by asking probing questions. However, do not parade your knowledge unsolicited, or show that you know more than the interviewer.

The future – Do they have one? Ask about the organization's future plans. You could put this question in the following manner: 'I appreciate that the future plans of your organization are probably confidential, but I wonder if you could say whether it will be expanding, bringing out new types of products or going into new areas'. The life of an organization falls into three phases.

1) Rapid growth from a small business
personnel are highly motivated
absence of 'red tape'
much innovation
resources stretched

2) Consolidation.
personnel becoming more interested in salary and

conditions rather than the job
'empire building'
creeping bureaucracy
generally good quality products and service

3) Decline.
market share being eroded
quality of service declining
financial crises
redundancies
political in-fighting among managers
personnel do little self-development

You need to find out which phase your prospective employer is at.

Double check – they may be lying Interviewers are not always honest about their own organization. The interviewer may say that it is the policy to promote from within. Later on, in the interview, you can ask what job your future superior was doing before his present one: you can then see if *he* was promoted from within or brought in from outside the organization. You are selling yourself, and the interviewer is selling his organization to you. When people sell they tend to exaggerate. Make certain that the interviewer does not exaggerate the benefits to you of joining his organization.

Will you have a budget? – 'Yes – but it's impossible!' If relevant, ask if you will be expected to work within a budget and if so how it is calculated – and if you will be consulted as to how it is arrived at. Ask for the budget figures of the department for the last three years. In this way you can see if it is static, expanding or contracting. You will also be able to assess whether there is an adequate budget for the work expected. Many bright-eyed managers and administrators with great ideas have come to grief because they have been thwarted by a too restrictive budget.

Draw out any objections to yourself You must draw out from the interviewer all possible objections which he may have about you doing the job. This may be difficult because people rarely tell you why they do not want to employ you. You must keep digging away at the interviewer until you get to the root of any objection.

I help others! Show that you are a useful person to employ because you help others in their jobs. Examples of this attitude are:

- helping new employees or trainees
- helping colleagues in critical situations
- producing easy to read guides for others – if a specialist
- helping the careers of those reporting to you
- getting involved with other peoples' problems

If these points do not apply to you, then change your ways now, and make a positive effort to help others.

THE KEY QUESTIONS

'Do you have any reservations about my doing the job?' At the end of the interview you must ask this question. If there are any reservations you can now counter them. If you do not clear up these reservations in the interviewer's mind you will stand little chance of getting the job. However, if you can counter the reservations and then repeat the question you must stand an excellent chance of getting the job. For example: 'Yes – we think you could do the job but are worried that you have not had people working directly under you'. You may be able to counter this as follows: 'It is true that in my present job, I have not had people reporting directly to me. However, I was a part-time fireman for five years and had four people working under me then, so that I do have a fair amount of experience of handling people. Are there any other doubts about me doing the job?' The interviewer may then reply 'No, I don't think so. When can you start?'

Go on then – ask for the job You must ask for the job, not directly of course. Say something like the following: 'After discussing the job and your company with you, Mr Smith, I am certainly very interested and keen to join you, and if you did make me an offer, provided, of course, we could agree on salary, I would be happy to accept'.

OK – So why should we hire you? At the end of the interview you may be asked the question: 'Why should we give you the job in preference to the other applicants?'
You must reply as follows
'I, of course, know nothing of the other applicants, but after discussing the job with you today, I am confident that I could make a success of it'.

Then *briefly* go through the ways in which you meet their requirements without elaborating and *finish*. Never compare yourself with any of the other candidates or be drawn into any kind of discussion about them. Go through your reasons why you are suited for the job and convince them that you are the person who meets their requirements and will do the job.

The green light question Towards the end of the interview you may be asked one of the following questions:

do you really think that you have enough experience?
do you think you are ready for this additional responsibility?
don't you think you are rather young/old for this job?

You may interpret the question as your failure to get the job and so lose heart thus giving a reply which throws doubt into the mind of the interviewer. *You could not be more wrong.* This question is a signal that the interviewer does think that you are the right person, he is ready to offer it to you, but just wants you to reassure him. Have an answer ready which will reassure the interviewer of your competence. With this knowledge you will now recognize this green light and give a confident reply which will ensure your success.

Salary – go high – You can always come down When the question of salary arises – ask for the highest possible. Even if the job as advertised quotes a salary, ask for at least 10 per cent more. If you have convinced the interviewer that you can do the job you can probably get him to offer more than the original figure. Ask when your salary will be reviewed. Try to get a review after six months. After all, if they are willing to pay you a salary knowing little about you, they should give you a raise if they are satisfied with you after six months work.

Don't play hard to get Don't play hard to get – interviewers won't stand for it. By applying for the job in question you have shown that you are interested in getting it – so don't pretend that you are not. Negotiating a good deal is largely a question of attitude and phrasing. If you are trying to get more money don't say:
'If you offered me another 10 per cent on the salary I may be tempted to accept your offer'
Instead say
'The job you are offering is definitely worth at least another 10 per cent on the salary especially for a person with my qualifications, experience and ability to get things done. Don't you agree!'

Do not give the impression that you are playing one employer off against another. Give the impression that you want the job but know how much you are worth.

CHECKLIST OF POSSIBLE INTERVIEW QUESTIONS

Think about the following questions and prepare answers to them

1) Where does your main experience lie?
2) What are your main responsibilities in your present job?
3) How much time do you spend on each aspect of your job?
4) What are the main problem areas of your job?
5) What do you do particularly well?
6) What does your boss think of you?
7) What are your career objectives?
8) Why do you want to leave your present employer?
9) Are there any people you find difficulty working with?
10) What do you want to be doing in five years' time?
11) What are your strong points?
12) What are your weak points?
13) Why should we hire *You*?

Do not forget to be ready for the green light question

8 Group and panel interviews

GROUP INTERVIEWS

Do not be put off All the candidates together may be asked to discuss a given topic whilst they are observed by several assessors. Group interviews are difficult to assess and control but one is sometimes required as a preliminary to the main interview. Their purpose is to help gain an overall impression of how you react with other people, to predict your reaction in a similar work environment. You will not be selected for a job solely on your performance at a group interview. If you do particularly badly compared with the other candidates then this will obviously weight heavily against you. Do not try to be much better than the average, either, since by so doing you may act unnaturally and again score badly. By the very nature of these interviews you cannot plan out in advance what you will do or say. Therefore, you must be yourself and try to appear about average.

The assessors will be marking you on certain negative and positive qualities, so bear these in mind. Examples of these qualities follow.

Negative qualities – work on these if they apply to you! Analyse yourself for the following negative qualities and try hard to counter them.

shyness
failure to talk
stubbornness
unable to take criticism
hogging the conversation
criticizing others
interrupting other speakers
condescension
patronizing others

pompousness
introducing irrelevancies
arguing

Positive qualities – concentrate on these Be aware of these qualities which will make a good impression with your assessors.

leadership, by trying to keep any discussion constructive
sticking to the point of questions
getting others to talk and contribute their bit
contributing your share to the discussion
talking from experience rather than in abstracts

Say your bit early and often Make sure you contribute early by saying something – anything. Keep interjecting your comments to make sure you keep in the discussion. If you fail to speak up early you will find it very difficult to come in later, even though you have something worthwhile to say.

The longer you leave saying your bit the harder it becomes to contribute.

Public speaking – prepare Group interviews often require some public speaking. You may be required to stand up and give a short talk to the group. Favourite subjects are:

your present job
your life
your hobbies

Practise each of these in anticipation of this session. The guide lines for giving these talks are as follows:

keep to the point
look at all members of the audience
use examples from real life rather than talk in the abstract
involve the audience if possible by asking questions
do not use technical terms or jargon
use your arms to help animate your talk
move around – do not stand stiffly in one spot
open strongly by memorizing your first sentence
close concisely by memorizing your last sentence

There is no time off Do not think that you are not being assessed at coffee or meal breaks. These may be just as important as the group interview itself. Do not be tricked into talking too candidly or openly about yourself. Just as in a formal interview you would think carefully, before answering a question, so on these occasions you must do the same. Do not fall into the trap of thinking you will impress people by being 'open' or frank. You are still 'under the spotlight' so treat the situation as if it were an actual interview.

Be friendly Chat to the other candidates. Find out their backgrounds and why they want the job. This will help to relax you and you may be able to gleen some useful information about the job or the company. Do not be put off by the apparent confidence of the other candidates. People always look more self assured than they feel!

PANEL INTERVIEWS

You may be interviewed by a panel of people, either prior to your main interview or as your sole interview. Organizations which are accustomed to collective responsibility and to committees favour panel interviews. For example, Civil Service, Local Government, academic bodies. Industry, on the other hand, is used to executives taking individual responsibility and favours separate interviews by lone interviewers, each interview following the previous one.
Panel interviews tend to be more serious but have advantages and disadvantages.

Advantages

- responsibilty for picking the successful candidate is shared
- only one session is required
- prejudice and subjectivity are reduced
- members can correct each other on matters of fact

Disadvantages

- one member can overshadow the other members
- the candidate can be overawed
- haphazard questioning by inexperienced members can upset candidates
- the formality of the occasion can be restrictive in getting the candidate to 'open up'
- the panel members may be more concerned with impressing, or scoring points off each other than evaluating the candidates

Points to watch Make sure that you look at all members of the panel when you are answering questions. To counteract a person who may be trying to monopolize the interview, give very full answers with follow-up questions when other members of the panel speak to you. However, do not be rude to the monopolizer because the other members will resent that too. Because the atmosphere is formal and since there are several interviewers it may not be practical to address the panel members by name. Occasional use of 'Gentlemen', 'Ladies', 'Sir', or 'Madam' may seem old fashioned but will be appreciated by the panel members.

Because you will be sitting further away from some members, than at a normal interview *talk a little louder.*

9 After the interview

After the interview, write back and thank the company for the interview and say that you are still very interested in the vacancy. If there are any important points which you failed to bring up at the interview, mention them in your letter. Some applicants use interviews and job offers to extract rises in salary from their own organizations and would not accept an offer, even if made. You must convince the interviewer that you are sincere, this letter will do just that and could tip the scales in your favour.

Send the letter by first class post and write and post it on the evening of the interview so that it reaches the company without delay. Consider writing a draft of this letter before your interview, you can rewrite it on the premises and post in the nearest post box.

Keep your promises The world is full of people who do not keep promises. Show the interviewer that you do what you say. Send the names of referees or additional specimens of work with your letter of thanks. This should be sent by first class mail, and never delivered by hand as the interviewer will think that you are just a little too keen – maybe even desperate to get the job.

Other offers If you have attended several interviews and an offer results from one of these previous ones, then you must decide which job you really want and not play one organization off against another. You may lose both offers if you do. If you still hope to be made and accept an offer by your latest interview, then ring up the interviewer's *secretary* and arrange to see the interviewer on a 'matter of urgency'. You can then discuss the situation with him in person. Never discuss this over the telephone. (Hence the need to ring the secretary and not the interviewer). Try not to divulge to the secretary why you are ringing.

By following this procedure you will get a good idea of the chance of being offered a job. You will not be wasting time waiting for news. If necessary be direct, ask the interviewer whether he will be making you an offer or not!

Congratulations – you have been offered the job Write back immediately, even if you were offered the job at the interview, to confirm that you accept and also to confirm the important points such as work location, salary, position in the company, general responsibilities, starting date, use of company car, etc. Ask the company to confirm to you in writing that you have understood the above points correctly. *Only when you receive their reply,* give in your notice to your present employer. There are many people who have been enticed into a job with promises, for example, with the promise of a company car, only to find too late that this was a 'misunderstanding'. An example of the letter which you should write back is given at the end of this chapter.

Give in your notice gracefully Never be tempted to settle old scores. Be as pleasant as possible even to those you hate. Leave behind you a good reputation – bad reputations have a nasty habit of catching up on you.

You are still on trial During the first six months of your new job you will still be on trial. If you fail to live up to your promises your future prospects will rapidly fade, or you could be asked to leave. Consider this period also as a time when your new employer is on trial as far as you are concerned. Is it living up to promises made at the interview?

Why not defer moving home for say six months until you are certain of your position. Use this time to get to know the new area, for schools, residential areas, etc. *Do not be in a hurry to move.*

Learn by your mistakes If you fail to get a particular job then review your performance at the interview by asking yourself the following questions:

- Was the job what you really wanted anyway?
- Did you get over your examples of how you meet the job requirements?
- Did you ask the right questions?
- Which questions did you answer badly?
- Did you ask 'Have you any reservations about me doing the job? ' – what was the reply.
- Did your qualifications match the requirements?
- Was your experience good enough?
- Did you get on well with the interviewer?

If possible ring up the interviewer and ask him who was offered the job and why you were not.

Make a note of your conclusion and put it in your job file. Before your next interview get out your file and read the notes from the previous interviews.

43 Cumberland Road,
Stockley,
Cardiff.

19th May, 1976

Mr A.P. Stone,
The Personnel Manager,
Brooks and Co. Ltd.,
45 Upper Link Road,
Oxford.

Dear Mr Stone,

Vacancy – Marketing Manager

Thank you for your offer to employ me as Marketing Manager as contained in your letter of 18th May 1976.

Various points were raised at interview and I should just like you to confirm that I have understood them correctly.

1. I will be based at your Oxford office on a salary of £10,000 per annum with a 10 per cent bonus for achieving a specified target volume of sales over a year.

2. I will report to Mr S. Dixon, the Managing Director and will be responsible for all sales in the U.K.

3. I will have the use of a company car (Rover 3500 or equivalent) for all business and private use.

Assuming that you can confirm the points above I shall be very happy to accept your offer and start work on August 1st 1976.

Yours sincerely,

H.L. Boyce

10 Assessing the job

Any job should be assessed under the following two headings:
1) Working conditions, salary and benefits.
2) Job satisfaction.

WORKING CONDITIONS

It is important to understand working conditions, salary and benefits from the start, although they are not of paramount importance. Never dwell on these points at the interview and, if possible, do not discuss them until you are sure that you will be offered the job.

Job level Find out if you will be assigned to a specific job level or grade, and if this level carries a salary range with it. What is the minimum and maximum salary for this range? How can you get promoted to the next level, how long does it normally take at one level before one is considered for promotion to the next? What proportion of people at your level can expect promotion to the next level (1) with five years and (2) before retirement?

Salary and fringe benefits Find out how salaries are arrived at. Ideally they should be determined on a scale according to job level, performance and experience. How are salary reviews carried out and are they annual? When comparing one job against another, not only salary, but also the value of additional benefits, must be taken into account.

- Is there free life assurance?
- Are there sickness and accident benefits, and are they adjusted for rises in the cost of living?
- Is the pension fund free or contributory or both?
- Is the pension adjusted for rises in the cost of living?
- Is a car provided – what are the conditions of use?

- What holidays are given?
- Is a bonus paid; what was its value for the last 3 years?
- Is assistance given for relocation to the new job?

Working conditions

- What are the normal working hours?
- How long will it take you to travel to work each day?
- Is there free transport to work?
- Is there free uniform or special clothing?
- Will you have your own office?
- Will you have or share a secretary?
- Is overtime expected and paid for?
- Is weekend working required?
- Is travel frequent?

JOB SATISFACTION

In order for you to be happy and derive satisfaction from your job, the following conditions must exist. (In the end, these are far more important than salary and fringe benefits).

The ability to do the job You must find out enough about the job to convince yourself that you can do it – with training if necessary. *Do not underestimate yourself.* People have a tremendous ability to grow into bigger jobs.

Scope for learning To be interesting, a job should be a continuous process of learning. When you stop learning most jobs lose their interest. Is there scope in the job to keep learning new things or to receive new responsibilities? Is the company keen on re-educating its people? Does it run its own courses or send people on external courses? You should discuss your education schedule, if appropriate, for the first year.

Controlling one's work Each person should be given the means to continually assess his own work and progress. Will you be given enough scope to correct your own mistakes? To assess and control one's own work quality promotes 'pride in the job'. What are the criteria for measuring your performance, and will your salary be linked to it?

Movement inside the organization Is there scope within the organization to do a different job after a few years? This need not be a promotion but just the ability to offer you work in a different field. After a few years you may want a change and a move to another employer could be expensive, particularly in terms of lost pension rights, etc.

No promises – please No account should be taken of any promises given. For example – that a much larger salary or a car will be given in two years' time. Most promises of this kind never materialize. You must always demand the rate for the job – never accept less.

Check up with your future colleagues If you feel unsure of your prospective employer, ask to chat to some of your prospective colleagues. Concentrate on asking specific questions from which you will be able to judge the prospective employer rather than just asking them whether he is a good employer to work for. (They will invariably say yes). Ask these questions:

- How long have you worked for this employer?
- How long have you been in this particular job?
- How many hours overtime did you work last week?
- How many times have you stopped late during the last month?
- When was your salary last reviewed?
- How does your salary compare with what you could get in other similar organizations?
- How often do you discuss your job with your manager?
- How many hours a day do you spend on administration?
- Which decisions does your manager have to approve?
- What are the main problems of the job?
- How many of your colleagues have left in the last two years?
- Are you looking for another job now?
- Is the organization expanding, static or declining?
- Have there been any redundancies in the last five years?
- How many new people have been taken on in the last two years?
- What do you think of the products or services of the organization?
- Does the customer get value for money?

11 Your first job (for school leavers and students)

Do not worry about getting the 'right' job at your first attempt – the chances of finding it first time are small. Most people change their jobs several times particularly during the early part of their careers. Indeed, there are advantages in changing your job a few times. You will gain a greater breadth of experience and will not be so psychologically dependent on your employer, and if you have to change later in life (e.g. due to redundancy) it will be easier for you. However, do not become a 'job hopper' by changing your job every year or less. You should aim to stay at least 3 years in any job to get worthwhile experience.

Whatever job you find yourself in you must do every aspect of it as well and as conscientiously as possible. You will only gain promotion or get a better job when you can prove that *you do your existing job well.*

SELECTING A JOB

Getting advice Most schools have a careers officer, usually a teacher who does the job on a part-time basis. This person is there to give advice about applying for jobs, which organizations to contact, organizing visits, etc, but not to tell you which career to go in for, although a discussion about this would be worthwhile. Discuss with your parents your plans and get them to visit the head teacher and careers officer. The school will then feel more committed to helping you.

Colleges and universities may have an appointments board which provides the same function as a careers officer but also arranges actual job interviews with employers, on the college premises. Use the appointments board to get information and to discuss possible career opportunities.

Keep studying Whatever your first job is, aim to continue studying. This may be required by the job itself – to get more qualifications, but even if this is not required then study anyway. This will give you a greater breadth of knowledge which could be useful in your present job and which could tip the scales for you when going after your next one. If possible use your studies to complement your work. A typist could study bookkeeping, a scientist, metalwork, a production engineer, financial planning, etc.,

Find out what evening courses there are in your area, and what is available by correspondence course. By making this use of part of your free time you will certainly increase your chances of success if you change your job again.

Get work experience in your holidays Try to get some job in your holidays, even with little or no pay. This will stand you in good stead. Employers prefer employing someone who has some positive work experience.

After each holiday job ask the person for whom you were working to write you a short testimonial – you may be embarrassed to ask but will rarely get refused.

Select a job which will help you when you start your career. This does not mean it has to be in the same field as your career, in fact, it is better if it is not, but in a field which will give you experience which will be useful but which you would not have otherwise have got.

Career	*Suggested holiday job*
Architect	building site labouring
Linguist	travel office
Mechanical engineer	sales office
Teacher	personnel department in industry
Computer programmer	general commercial office

Do not wait for holiday jobs to be advertized, write to employers and tell them why you want a holiday job in a certain field. For example, by working in a general commercial office you will more readily appreciate the procedures you will later meet as a computer programmer. In your letter of application for the full-time job you will mention your holiday jobs. Put your testimonials in your job file and take them to your interview.

Other interests are important For you, your interests outside your studies are important; since you have no previous work experience, this is one of the yardsticks which a prospective employer has of

judging your initiative and your ability to get along with people. Particularly valuable are those activities in which you had some organizing function, and where you had to get along with and work with others. Examples of activities particularly useful are as follows: school sports team, school prefect, debating society, school/college magazine, scout/guide clubs, youth groups, voluntary service
Note: Keep off the subject of political activities as this could set up a strong prejudice against you. The membership of extreme political parties could bar you from some jobs. If you are still at school or college prepare for the future by taking part now in some activity outside your studies. This should be where you are meeting and working with other people.

LETTER OF APPLICATION

Because you have little actual experience in the particular job or career for which you are applying, your letter of application must project a positive image of yourself through the things which you have done. You can apply in your own handwriting. However use a large plain sheet of white paper (not small notepaper). Place a lined sheet underneath so that your writing is neat and even. Leave a large margin at each side of the paper and set out your letter as shown in the examples in this book. Print your name beneath your signature, if this is unreadable.

If the advertisement just says 'apply to. . .' then you could go along in person without writing a letter. This will enable you to get a good idea of the place and the people working there.

Read the specimen letter on page 85 and see how it provides the following examples of fulfilling requirements of the job.

Job requirement	*Example*
academic attainment	'O' levels and 'A' levels
team spirit	member of choir
leadership	group leader
healthy and able-bodied	crewing catamaran
interest in people	part-time jobs
initiative	learning to drive and car maintenance
maturity	wanting to start work rather than studying for the sake of it

Get your letter checked After writing your letter of application, get a teacher or parent to check it for spelling mistakes, punctuation and grammar. However, provided you have adhered to the principles in this book do not be persuaded to change the style of your letter, e.g., by including extra personal details about yourself, etc.,

SPECIMEN LETTER – APPLYING TO JOIN A POLICE FORCE

45 Upper Court,
Gloucester.
12th January, 1978

Mr F.S. Cooper,
The Chief Constable,
Bristol County Police,
44 High Street,
Bristol.

Dear Sir,

I am writing to you because I would like to join your Police Force after I have taken my 'A' Levels later this year.

Apart from working for 'O' Levels (six passes) and three 'A' Levels I am a member of my school choir which has given concerts on radio, television and in the USA. I also support a national interdenominational organization for young people, and with members of this organization crewed a catamaran for holidays sailing along northern France and Brittany. As a Group Leader I take a class of ten to thirteen year olds on Sundays.

I am very interested in those activities which involve meeting and working with people and the part-time jobs which I have had, have been working in a supermarket and various shops.

During the past year I have learnt to drive and can do simple car maintenance. I would like to pursue this interest of driving in the police.

After I have taken my 'A' Levels I want to get started on my career rather than go to college, and I think that life in the police force will provide the kind of work which is interesting and rewarding.

Yours faithfully,

A.A. Brown (Miss)

Personal qualities are all important Since you have little actual job experience, personal qualities are all important. You must place much emphasis on projecting your personal qualities and convincing the prospective employer on the following points:

punctuality
ability to work hard
willingness to absorb training
ability to learn
ability to get on with people
self discipline
loyalty
adaptability to change
initiative
presentable appearance
good manners

Because the general impression, which the interviewer gets of you is the biggest single factor in determining whether you will be offered a job – you must be neatly and soberly dressed. Girls – wear a dress or skirt, boys – a suit. You must *never* wear jeans. Occasionally one hears of people advising school leavers that it would be acceptable to appear for interview casually dressed, for example, in jeans, etc. You must disregard this advice. If you cannot be bothered to dress properly for interview then you insult the person giving the interview. No matter what people say or what the general fashion in casual clothes is: **A smart and neat appearance increases your chances of being successful.**

Again, because of your lack of experience you will be more likely to be subjected to tests of various types. Get yourself a book of tests and practise.

Why employ you? Even if you have had the benefit of the finest education, this does not *entitle* you to a job. Jobs are created by industrious people starting businesses and wanting to employ others, or by the State or local authority (which is the rest of the population) requiring a service. You have to convince an employer that you are worth employing viz. that the value of the service which you will render will be greater than the salary which you will be paid. You must convince the employer that you will work hard and be ready to change the work you do, if necessary, in order to justify your salary. People who are unwilling to adapt to change or adjust to new circumstances (think that the world owes them a living) do not deserve jobs and will generally not get satisfaction from any job. You must project the right attitude; skills and qualifications can always be added later, but attitudes are more difficult to change.

What do you read? Students and school leavers are frequently asked which books they read. If you don't read much then do not try and pretend that you do – you will be found out! It is better to pass the question off by saying that you prefer more practical activities such as model making, sport, etc., rather than bluffing your way through.

Questions may also be asked about current affairs. To prepare for this, read thoroughly at least one newspaper daily during your job hunting period.

There is the boring and routine in everything Most jobs have an element of the boring, routine type of work. Do not be discouraged by this. The art of enjoying work is to get through the boring and routine as quickly and efficiently as possible and get on to the interesting aspects. When you can complete the routine work efficiently and cheerfully, you will be ready for more responsibility.

If the topic of 'interesting' work comes up show the interviewer that you want interesting work to do but realize that you will have to do a proportion of boring or repetitive activities – filing, writing reports, filling in forms, etc., but that you will be able to take this in your stride. You will gain high marks for adopting this mature approach. You should think out your long term aims, not only so that you can progress in the right direction but also as this is likely to be a recurring question at your job interviews throughout your working life. However you should always stress that your primary objective is to do your *present job* as well as possible.

Questions to ask To evaluate how seriously the employer takes his responsibility for training school leavers and other young people, ask questions along the following lines:

- Is there a good training scheme for school leavers and apprentices?
- Are text books and tuition fees paid for?
- Are days off allowed to continue study at college?
- Is there a training manager?
- Is there a system of job rotation so that different and varied experience can be gained?
- Will training consist of 'sitting with Ada', that is watching an experienced person working but with little actual formal instruction?
- Has the employer a well thought out and carefully planned training scheme?
- Of the school leavers taken on five years ago, how many are still with the company? Anything over 70 per cent is good, under 30 per cent is poor
- Do not discuss promotion, etc., too deeply, as first of all you have to convince the interviewer that you will work hard at the job which you will be offered and absorb the necessary training

12 Senior people

Fewer advertisements The majority of senior jobs whether in business or the professions are rarely advertised. You must rely on finding out about these jobs by other methods. However, be careful about your job hunting since if it became known to your present employer that you are looking around you could be sacked for disloyalty. If you are a director in a company your activity could also affect the company's share prices.

You can let the people who matter know that you are in the job market by discreetly spreading the word about.
Some useful contacts can be found among the following:

your club
your financial advisers
your merchant bank
your auditors
your bank manager
your solicitor

These people are in daily contact with other organizations and are in a good position to know of vacancies if they occur.

Press releases A carefully worded press release, through your Public Relation's advisers, can sometimes bring good results. For example:

> Jones Motors the specialist vehicle manufacturer has recently won their largest export order to supply 2,000 vehicles to a foreign government agency. This completes a five-year growth plan during which time the emphasis has been placed on export markets.

It is expected that the Financial
Director – Mr J. Smith having played
a major part in this phase, will be
looking for a challenging appointment
with a larger public company.

Executive search consultants These consultants specialize in helping senior people – chairmen, directors or senior managers. They also advise people on their long term career prospects by the use of counselling sessions.

Write them a short letter giving brief details of your history and achievements to date and expectations for the future.

Taking assignments It could be well worth your while to take a short assignment for say one year. Perhaps doing a specific job for another organization or a branch of government. In this way you will expose yourself to potential employers so that when the assignment is over you will have several offers to choose from.

Meet the wife The wives of senior people are also frequently interviewed – not formally at an office but over dinner. This is to assess your marital stability and your wife's ability to entertain business and professional acquaintances and clients. The atmosphere is informal and may take place in a restaurant or at your home. Make sure that your wife is properly briefed about your previous experience and has also memorized your examples of how you meet the job requirements.

You could, however, take the attitude that your wife is none of your employer's business and flatly refuse them meeting her. However, put this over tactfully, pointing out that if your wife was applying for a job you would not expect to be interviewed as well. Having made your decision as to whether your wife should be interviewed, stick to it; never change your mind. On balance, however, it is probably better to let your wife be interviewed if this is requested. Your wife should try *not* to impress. The most important quality being looked for is her ability to bring stability and provide a firm base to your life.

Can you make tough decisions? A senior person has to be able to take tough decisions which may affect the lives of many other people. The interviewers will be assessing your ability in this field by asking the following type of questions:

- How many people have you fired, demoted or moved?
- What innovations have you made?
- Were you responsible for your company moving to new fields?
- Can you cut back on under-productive assets?

- Can you go ahead with the right decision even though those around you say no?
- Have you altered the structure of organizations with which you have been associated?

Have you good contacts? Demonstrating that you have good contacts in industry, the professions, government or the financial institutions which would be of value to your potential employer will place you at an advantage over the other candidates. Selective name dropping will not come amiss, although it must not be over done.

Can you build a strong team? A manager or senior person should never think just in terms of things, tasks, figures, machines, etc., he should think primarily in terms of PEOPLE. No matter how good a person *you* are, a modern organization demands that the management team is sound. You must demonstrate that you know how to:

choose people
organize people
control people
motivate people

You must give the impression that you are:

People orientated

You must expect questions about those people reporting to you. Have you a good record for recruiting valuable people from outside your organization and for promoting promising people within it? Be prepared to discuss actual examples.

Are you a good communicator? The days are over when the boss could stay in his office shouting orders to subordinates. People at all levels need to know what is happening in their organization and what its attitude is to the issues of the day which affect it. Have you a good record of communicating with your employees? Can you demonstrate to an interviewer that you have? Do you regularly walk about your place of work meeting and talking to the ordinary employees?

What is your profit record? Increasingly senior people in business are measured on their profit record. Prepare a statement of the relevant figures over a period of three to five years, or longer if appropriate. Include with the statement any relevant press cuttings which demonstrate that your company is increasingly profitable and confident. This type of question can also be slanted to people working for government departments, local authorities and academic institutions by substituting the word budget for profit. You must be able to demonstrate that you can work within the budgets set and still give a satisfactory service, perhaps by innovating or using new techniques.

CHECKLIST FOR SENIOR PEOPLE

WRITE DOWN at least one example of how you meet the following points:

A SENIOR PERSON

can make *tough* decisions

generates *profit*

can work within *budget*

has good *contacts*

can build a strong *team*

communicates well

motivates others to excel

looks at the *future* through a telescope, not the present through a microscope

can say *yes* when everyone else says no

uses *time* effectively

always appears *confident*

delegates responsibility and authority

keeps people *informed* on matters of policy

constantly monitors the *structure* of the organization

manages *people* rather than jobs

is *cool* in crisis situations

works hard but is *effective*

Now memorize your examples

13 Women at work

There is no doubt that women sometimes meet special difficulties when job hunting in competition with men for jobs which are traditionally thought of as men's jobs. These difficulties can be broken down into two components:

1) A reputation which women in general are thought to have for certain attitudes or activities which are thought to have a detrimental effect on their performance at work.
2) Prejudice on the part of the interviewer which has been caused by some specific incident in the past.

In your letter of application for the job do not state that you are female either explicitly or by the way you sign your name. If you obtain an offer for an interview then in your letter of reply, just include your status after your name. This will enable the interviewer to know that you are a woman and he will not be taken by surprise at the interview.

Do not be tempted to take a different job, say as, a secretary or an assistant then think that you will work your way up to the job you should really have. This rarely works. You must enter an organization at the level which your experience and qualifications demand. Examples of special objections are discussed as follows:

Women get ill more often In addition to all the normal illnesses which men have, women are also subject to their own peculiar female disorders. Thus they are thought to take more time off for health reasons than men.

Counter this objection as follows:

1) Agree with the interviewer that women are subject to additional female disorders, but point out that men are also subject to take time off for reasons which occur more frequently in men, such as:

car accidents – it is a fact that a man is more liable to have a serious car accident than a woman
accidents from sport are more prevalent in men
alcoholism is more prevelant in men

With the above points you can at least throw doubts into the mind of the interviewer and he will think that perhaps this is not worth considering further.

2) If you have a good record of attendance this can be quoted. For example – that you have taken an average of only two days off per year for the last three years.

Women leave to get married or have children The interviewer may question whether it is worth hiring you when you may leave in a few years time to marry or have children. It is useless protesting that you intend neither of these things.

Counter this objection as follows:

1) Get the interviewer thinking about the positive contribution which you will make in the next, say two years.

2) Point out that women are less liable to 'job hopping' than men. If the interviewer hires a man then the probability that he will leave for another job after a few years is just as great as you leaving either to go to another job or to get married or have children

Women do not get on well with other women Women do have a reputation of not getting on well with other women either above or below them in an organization. This also applies to women managing men.

Counter this objection as follows:

1) Make it apparent, to the interviewer, that you are aware that there could be a problem in this area.

2) If possible, quote your experience in this area and reassure the interviewer that you have found no real problem to date. Better still say that you have met the problem but managed to deal with it, and explain how you did so.

Women are emotionally unstable Women occasionally meet the objection that they are emotionally unstable. This is likely to be caused by a personal experience of the interviewer of a woman who at a crisis, fell ill or burst into tears, etc.

Counter this objection as follows:

1) Demonstrate from your experience that you can handle crisis situations. Choose an example and show that you were able to adopt a cool approach, plan and resolve the problem.

2) Suggest that you have a stable relationship with your colleagues and that you are dependable.

The employer's paternalistic attitude This is caused by a concern for women that prevents the employer from allowing women to perform to their true potential. Examples of this attitude are:

1) An unwillingness to let a woman fall down on the job. Thus the really difficult assignments are not given to a woman for fear that she will fail.
2) 100 per cent effort is not asked for. Thus, overtime, weekend working, travelling, etc. is not required from the women employees but are from the men.

Counter this objection as follows:
In your present job, make sure that you are treated equally with the men of similar rank to you. Volunteer for extra work, difficult jobs, etc. if necessary. In your interview you can tactfully draw on these examples to reassure your interviewer.

Women don't delegate A common prejudice is that women are thought not to delegate sufficient work or responsibility to those under them. This may be because some, lacking in their own confidence, want to impress by showing how busy or indispensable they are.
Counter this objection as follows:
Give specific examples of how you delegate. If you are a supervisor or manager show that you understand that a major part of your job is to plan, delegate then review. Never imply that you are indispensable; but rather the opposite, that you always delegate sufficient aspects of your job for your department to carry on without you.

14 Final checklist of critical points

The advertisement
analyse the advertisement for the requirements needed to do the job, both *specific and hidden*

Letter of application
give no personal details and select from your experience only those items which are directly relevant to the job

Preparation for interview
memorize your examples of how your experience satisfies the job requirements

At the interview
Ask the following questions:

Where do I fit into the organization?
How will my performance be measured?
What is expected of me in the first year?
What happened to the last incumbent?
Have you any reservations about my doing the job?

Be ready to answer the following questions:

Why do you wish to leave your present job?
Why should we employ you?
The green light question?

At the end of the interview
ASK for the job

After the interview
Write and thank the company for the interview and confirm your continued interest in the job.

Memorize your examples of how you satisfy the job requirements

APPENDIX

PUBLICATIONS – CAREERS

Careers A – Z,	Collins.
Career Change,	Hobson Press (Cambridge) Ltd.
Career Choice,	Pan.
Career Encyclopedia,	Cassell.
Careers For School and College Leavers,	Haymarket Publishing.
Careers Guide,	H.M.S.O.
Directory of Opportunities For Graduates,	Haymarket Publishing.
The Annual Guide to Graduate Opportunities,	New Opportunity Press Limited.
The Good Job Guide,	New Opportunity Press Limited.

PUBLICATIONS – JOB-HUNTING ADVICE

Changing Your Job,	Kogan Press Limited.
Dismissal, Redundancy and Jobhunting,	Consumers Association.
Facing The Interview,	Unwin Paperbacks.
Finding Another Top Job,	Institute of Personnel Management.
How To Face That Interview,	Paperfont.
How to Get a Job,	Institute Of Personnel Management.
Starting Out,	John Goodchild Publishers.
The Survivors – Guide to Unemployment and Redundancy,	Corgi.

CAREER ADVICE AND GUIDANCE (GENERAL AND YOUNG PEOPLE)

Career Analysts,	Career House, 90 Gloucester Place, London W1.
Careers Counselling Services,	46 Ferry Road, London SW13.
Career Guidance Ltd.,	20 Bloomsbury Square, London WC1.
The Training Opportunities Scheme,	Manpower Services Commission, 180 High Holborn, London WC1.
Vocational Guidance Association,	7 Harley House, Upper Harley Street, London NW1.
Youth and Careers Service,	See under Local Education Authority in Yellow Pages.

CAREER ADVICE AND GUIDANCE (SENIOR PEOPLE, MANAGERS AND EXECUTIVES)

British Institute of Management,	Management House, Parker Street, London WC2.
Council For Career Development and Counselling,	Sundridge Park Management Centre, Plaistow Lane, Bromley, Kent.
Inter Exec.,	19 Charing Cross Road, London WC2.
Forty Plus Career Development Centre Ltd.,	High Holborn House, 49–51 Bedford Row, London WC1.
Frederick Chusid and Co. Ltd.,	35 Fitzroy Street, London W1.
Job Change Project,	School of Management Studies, The Polytechnic of Central London, 35 Marylebone Road, London NW1.
Percy Coutts and Co.,	140 Grand Buildings, Trafalgar Square, London WC2.

ADVICE ON SPECIFIC CAREERS

Association of Certified Accountants,
29 Lincoln's Inn Fields,
London, WC2A 3EE.

Institute of Cost and Management Accountants,
63 Portland Place,
London, W1N 4AB.

Royal Institute of British Architects,
66 Portland Place,
London, W1N 4AD.

Army Information Careers Centre,
Central Recuiting Depot,
5 Great Scotland Yard,
London SW1.

BBC Appointments Department,
Broadcasting House,
London, W1A 1AA.

Building Societies Institute,
Fanhams Hall,
Ware,
Hertfordshire.

Business Education Council,
Berkshire House,
168–173 High Holborn,
London, WC1V 7AG.

Institute of Chartered Accountants,
Chartered Accountants Hall,
Moorgate Place,
London, EC2P 2BJ.

Institute of Actuaries,
Staple Inn Hall,
High Holborn,
London, WC1V 7QJ.

Royal Aeronautical Society,
4 Hamilton Place,
London, W1V 0BQ.

Banking Information Services Careers Section,
10 Lombard Street,
London, EC3V 9AP.

Independent Broadcasting Authority,
70 Brompton Road,
London, SW3.

Building Industry Career Service,
82 New Cavendish Street,
London, W1M 8AD.

Institution of Chemical Engineers,
12 Gayfere Street,
London, SW1P 3HP.

Society of Chiropodists,
8 Wimpole Street,
London, W1M 8B4.

Institute of Civil Engineers,
Great George Street,
London, SW1P 3AA.

H.M. Coastguard,
Department of Trade,
Marine Division,
Sunley House,
90 High Holborn,
London, WC1 6LP.

Construction Industry Training Board,
Radnor House,
1272 London Road,
Norbury,
London, SW16 4EB.

Institution of Electrical and Electronic Technician Engineers,
2 Savoy Hill,
London, WC2R 0BS.

Society of Electronic and Radio Technicians,
57 Newington Causeway,
London, SE1.

Advisory Council for the Church's Ministry,
Church House,
Dean's Yard,
London, SW1P 3WZ.

Civil Service Commission,
Alencon Link,
Basingstoke,
Hampshire.

British Computer Society,
13 Mansfield Street,
London W1M 0BP.

General Dental Council,
37 Wimpole Street,
London, W1M 8DQ.

Society of Industrial Artists and Designers,
12 Carlton House Terrace,
London, SW1.

Institute of Electrical Engineers,
Savoy Place,
Victoria Embankment,
London, WC2R 0BL.

Engineering Careers Information Services,
54 Claredon Road,
Watford, WD1 1LA.

Forestry Commission,
231 Corstorphine Road,
Edinburgh, EG12 7AT.

British Hairdressing Apprenticeship Council,
Crossroads House,
165 The Parade,
Watford,
Herts.

British Horse Society,
British Equestrian Centre,
Stonleigh,
Kenilworth,
Warwickshire, CV8 2LR.

Hotel and Catering Industry Training Board,
Ramsey House,
Wembley Central Square,
Wembley,
Middlesex, HA9 7AP.

Board of Inland Revenue,
Director of Personnel,
New Court,
48 Carey Street,
London, WC2.

British Institute of Interior Design,
22–24 South Street,
Ilkeston,
Derbyshire, DE7 5QE.

British Furniture Trades Joint Industrial Council,
30 Harcourt Street,
London, W1H 2AA.

The Council for Education and Training of Health Visitors,
Clifton House,
Euston Road,
London, NW1.

Royal Horticultural Society,
80 Vincent Square,
London, SW1P 2PE.

Central London Industrial Training Association Limited,
241 Upper Street,
London, N1.

Chartered Insurance Institute,
The Hall,
20 Aldermanbury,
London, EC2V 7HY.

Institute of Journalists,
Bedford Chamber,
Covent Garden,
London, WC2E 8HA.

Law Society,
113 Chancery Lane,
London, WC2A 1PL.

Institute of Linguists,
24A Highbury Grove,
London, N5 2EA.

Institute of Marine Engineers,
76 Mark Lane,
London, EC3R 7JN.

British Medical Association,
BMA House,
Tavistock Square,
London, WC1.

Meteorological Office,
London Road,
Bracknell,
Berkshire.

Royal Naval Careers Service,
State House,
High Holborn,
London, WC1.

Nursing and Hospital Careers
Information Centre,
121–123 Edgware Road,
London, W2 2HX.

The Library Association,
7 Ridgmount Street,
London, WC1E 7AE.

Local Government Training Board
8 Arndale Centre,
Luton,
Bedfordshire, LU1 2TS.

Institute of Mechanical Engineers,
1 Birdcage Walk,
London, SW1H 9JJ.

Institute of Metallurgists,
Northway House,
High Road,
Whetstone, N20 9LW.

Institute of Mining and Metallurgy,
44 Portland Place,
London, W1N 4BR.

Royal College of Nursing,
1A Henrietta Place,
London, W1.

College of Occupational
Therapists,
20 Rede Place,
London, W2.

General Optical Council,
41 Harley Street,
London, W1N 2DJ.

Institute of Personnel
Management,
IPM House,
Camp Road,
Wimbledon,
London, SW19.

Royal Photographic Society,
The Octagon,
Milson Street,
Bath, BA1 1BN.

Police Recruiting Department,
Home Office,
6 Harrow Road,
London, WC2.

Probation Service,
Home Office,
73 Great Peter Street,
London, SW1.

RAF Careers Information
Office,
Kelvin House,
Cleveland Street,
London, W1.

College of Radiographers,
14 Upper Wimpole Street,
London, W1N 8BN.

Chartered Institute of Patent Agents,
Staple Inn Buildings,
High Holborn,
London, WC1V 7PZ.

Pharmaceutical Society of Great Britain,
1 Lambeth High Street,
London, SE1 7JN.

The Chartered Society of Physiotherapy,
14 Bedford Row,
London, W1R 4ED.

Prison Department,
Home Office,
89 Eccleston Square,
London, W1.

Institute of Quantity Surveyors,
98 Gloucester Place,
London, W1H 4AT.

British Railways Board
Recruitment and Training,
222 Marylebone Road,
London, NW1.

Institute of Chartered Secretaries and Administrators,
16 Park Crescent,
London, W1N 4AH.

College of Speech Therapists,
Harold Poster House,
6 Letchmere Road,
London, NW2 5BU.

Stock Exchange Employment and Careers Office,
The Stock Exchange,
London, EC2N 1HP.

Royal Institute of Chartered Surveyors,
12 Great George Street,
Parliament Square,
London, SW1P 3AD.

National Council for Voluntary Organisations,
26 Bedford Square,
London, WC1.

Central Council for Education and Training in Social Work,
Derbyshire House,
St Chad's Street,
London, WC1.

Institute of Statisticians,
36 Churchgate Street,
Bury St Edmunds,
Suffolk, IP33 1RD.

Institute of Structural Engineers,
11 Upper Belgrave Street,
London, SW1X 8BH.

Royal College of Veterinary Surgeons,
32 Belgrave Square,
London, SW1.